CHINA
INDO CH
MALAYA

This edition first published
in Great Britain in 2009
by the Political Cartoon Society.

ISBN 0-9549008-2-0

British Library Cataloguing
in Publication Data.

A CIP catalogue record for this book
can be obtained from the British
Library.

Book design by Bruce Nivison.

Printed and bound in Malta by
Gutenberg Press.

ILLINGWORTH

Political cartoons from the Daily Mail 1939–69

Timothy S Benson
Foreword by mac

Leslie Gilbert Illingworth 1902–79

Foreword

For as long as I can remember I have been an avid doodler and cartoon watcher. My parents were *Daily Mail* readers and when I was quite young the day could only start properly for me after I had read the strip cartoons - Flook by Wally Fawkes and *Rip Kirby* by Alex Raymond. Then it was quickly over to the political cartoon to marvel at the drawings by Leslie Illingworth. He was my hero; the ultimate master of this craft and to my mind the best political cartoonist of the 20th century.

I never dreamt back then that I'd ever meet the great man, but when I did he turned out to be a wonderfully generous and friendly man, although a little forgetful at times. We went out to lunch twice within a short period and spent a great deal of time chatting about work and politics, but the next time we met he thought that I worked in the picture library and was quite surprised to learn that I was struggling to make a name as a cartoonist.

Illingworth was small in stature with great bushy eyebrows, a low forehead and a very prominent lower jaw. "I'm the missing link, Boyo," he would proclaim, "Phrenologists queue up to measure my skull. Got any bananas?" Despite this description of himself he was loved and admired by both sexes. He exuded warmth, generosity and humour and was very rarely seen sitting in a restaurant or bar alone. This gregarious nature often made him late for deadlines, putting the page planners and editors into a panic whilst he remained totally unflustered. "Nearly finished, Boyo," he'd lie into the phone, picking up a blank piece of art board before making a start on a beautifully composed political cartoon.

Leslie also drew the lead cartoon each week for *Punch* magazine and would attend the lunches that were held each Wednesday. On the huge table there would often be a bowl of hard boiled eggs and before leaving Leslie would stuff his pockets with eggs then give them to an old tramp who lived in a doorway opposite the *Punch* office. This was a regular occurrence and when the tramp saw Leslie approaching he'd bounce up and down with excitement. "Eggies!" he'd cry, "Eggies!" Once on a cold day I saw the tramp sitting in his doorway wearing a really nice coat. He told me it was given to him by the Eggyman.

Wally Fawkes 'TROG', who took over the political cartoon slot in the *Daily Mail* when Illingworth retired, remembers going to see Leslie, who was ill and in hospital. It was visiting time and each bed in the long ward was surrounded by the patients' relatives and friends. After they'd chatted for a while Leslie said, "Hang on, Wally. Won't be a tick", then popped out of bed totally naked, trotted past all the gawping visitors, did what he had to do, then sauntered back down the ward into bed, oblivious to the stares. "Now, where were we?" he asked.

Illingworth was unique, a one off, a genius. I have on the wall of my study a drawing of his that appeared in *Punch* magazine, which he signed for me. It is a dramatic scene drawn in the late 1970s of a Frankenstein monster representing the wild-cat strikers of the time being totally out of control and wading through the wreckage of industry whilst tiny law and order figures try to restrain him.

It is a wonderful piece of artwork that is a masterpiece of scraperboard technique. This means that the artist starts work with a completely black board and creates the drawing by scraping the board with a sharp implement to reveal white lines underneath. The result is amazing and such was Illingworth's ability the effect it gives is that he merely scratched away all the black to reveal the superb drawing that was already there under the surface. I will treasure it forever.

I'm so glad that Tim Benson has written so entertainingly about Illingworth. He was a truly great artist, a warm and witty human being and a wonderful example to follow for any would be cartoonist.

Stan McMurtry 'MAC'

Preface

I am proud, albeit somewhat mystified, of the fact that I am the only person to have put on an exhibition of Leslie Illingworth's cartoons in this country, held at the Political Cartoon Gallery in September 2004. One other exhibition of his work, apart from a travelling wartime one, was put on in the United States in Boston in 1970, which Illingworth attended in person. It is amazing to think that a great cartoonist such as Illingworth became forgotten so quickly after his death in 1979, regardless of the fact that today many of his cartoons have gained iconic status in historical and political textbooks. Illingworth was one of the most prolific cartoonists of the 20th century as well as one of its finest illustrators too. Yet nothing has been written on him apart from a sorry excuse for a post-doctoral thesis at the University of Kent in 2001, which I came across during my research on Illingworth. I hope this book will deservedly right that wrong.

This book published in May 2009, I am pleased to say, coincidentally commemorates a number of Illingworth anniversaries. The first being the seventieth anniversary of Illingworth starting at the *Daily Mail*; the second being the fortieth anniversary of his retirement from the *Daily Mail*; and thirdly the thirtieth anniversary of his death.

Timothy S. Benson May 2009

Acknowledgements

I am very grateful to the following for their help and assistance with this book:

The National Library of Wales/Llyfrgell Genedlaethol Cymru for giving permission to use the cartoons that the Library supplied for this book. The National Library of Wales has an archive of approximately 5,000 original cartoons given to them by Illingworth and I would like to thank Dr Rhidian Griffiths, Nia Mai Daniel, Scott Waby, Simon Evans, Rob Phillips and Iwan ap Dafydd at the Library for all their help along the way. Of course, Leslie being a very generous man, all the best original cartoons were given away, so I would therefore also like to thank cartoonists Les Gibbard and Draper Hill as well as Jim Hall and Ian Mackenzie for providing me with excellent reproductions of cartoons that are not part of the National Library of Wales' Collection. Leslie Illingworth's nephews, Richard Illingworth and Julian Lewis as well as cartoonists Wally Fawkes, Frank Dickens and Bernard Cookson who were all very helpful in supplying anecdotes as well as many of the photographs that appear in this book. Bruce Nivison as per normal for design and layout of the book. I would like to thank Peter Micklethwait and Martin Haslam for their generous sponsorship. Stan McMurtry 'MAC' for his amusing and insightful foreword. Danny Howell at Solo Syndication for allowing the Political Cartoon Society copyright permission to use the cartoons that appear in the book. Geoff Fordham for his assistance in the writing of the captions. Joyce Walker and Julie Reichman for their proofreading skills.

Leslie Gilbert Illingworth could be described as the last great penman in the line of English Social Satirists, starting with Hogarth, traceable through the biting and rambunctious broadsides of Rowlandson, Gillray and Cruikshank, continuing to the more moderate social comments of Leech, Tenniel, Keene and Phil May. It is fairly safe to assume that when the history of cartoon and caricature comes to be written, the name of Illingworth will have a valued place in the tradition of great political satire of this century, along with Will Dyson, Low, Giles, Vicky and Osbert Lancaster.

Keith Mackenzie, *The Artist*, June 1969

Richard Frederick Illingworth, Leslie's father, was a quantity surveyor who was engaged in dock construction work in the thriving seaport of Barry, in the Vale of Glamorgan, South Wales. At the time, the Barry Railway brought coal down from the South Wales Valleys to the Barry dock. The coal trade was making Barry the largest coal exporting port in the world. Richard came from an old Yorkshire family that had settled in Wales in the 1890's. His wife Helen, a former schoolteacher, was born of Scottish parents but brought up in Hull. The Illingworth's were married in Cardiff in 1896 and soon settled in Barry. On 2 September 1902, a year after the retirement of the 19th century's greatest cartoonist, Sir John Tenniel, Helen gave birth to a son who they named Leslie Gilbert Illingworth. She had already given birth to her first child, a boy named Vivian Richard Illingworth, in 1899 and in 1905, Phyllis Jean Illingworth was born. In that same year, requiring larger accommodation, the Illingworth family moved out of Barry and settled 17 miles away in the village of St Athan.

First surviving work. This was drawn by Illingworth when he was four. The drawing was found by his Aunt Lucy at Cardiff.

Leslie Illingworth's aptitude for drawing was first noticed at the age of four. As a young boy his physique was small and undeveloped in comparison with other boys. This naturally led to him to being diffident and shy with people, and Illingworth's outlet for self-expression was seen neither by kicking a ball around the back streets of Barry nor by getting up to mischief like most other boys of his age, but through a growing love for drawing. Illingworth spent all of his spare time drawing, especially caricature. His first attempts at caricature were encouraged by the village blacksmith in St. Athan, a man by the name of Evan Hopkins, known familiarly as 'Lanto the Forge'. As Illingworth later remembered:

> He started me off as a caricaturist, for the first public drawing I ever did was of Tom Llewellyn, Glebe Farm, with his arm in a sling. I did it on the tarred door of the forge with a lump of chalk that Lanto gave me.

When Illingworth was seven, the local vicar took a liking to him after he also had been drawn on the door of the blacksmith's forge. After that the vicar allowed Illingworth to copy from the large range of illustrated books he kept at the vicarage, including volumes of *Punch* in his private collection. He later recalled:

> I used to copy the drawings in his books. I didn't have art lessons, you see. I got by.

At his primary school, his teacher was very concerned that he would draw on all his exercise and text books. She enquired of her superiors what she should do about it and was told to let him draw on whatever he wished. His talent was obvious to everyone even at that early age. Apart from drawing, Illingworth developed an early love of nature and animals and subsequently spent a lot of his childhood working on nearby farms. "I always wanted to be a farmer," he later said, "but I won a scholarship to the local grammar school." Here at Barry County Boys' Grammar School he befriended Ronald Niebour who, coincidentally, was also later to become a cartoonist at the *Daily Mail* working under the pseudonym 'NEB'. Niebour joined the *Daily Mail* as a pocket cartoonist in 1938, a year before Illingworth.

Barry County School drawn by Illingworth in 1934

At 15, Illingworth obtained another scholarship, this time to the Cardiff Art School. He was proud of the fact that despite his parents not being wealthy he had benefited from a first class education, entirely due to the scholarships he had won:

> Here I am. A poor boy with no real influence and yet because I have taken advantage of scholarships, my education had cost me nothing. I have been a 'scholarship' man all the way through from the start.

At Cardiff Art School, he won a gold medal for drawing and had four topical cartoons published in the school's magazine, *Pen and Pencil*. Illingworth realised he had a natural talent for cartooning and saw that his next step was to get a foot in the door of a newspaper office - in his own words - "in any capacity". He asked his father if he could help, and, by some considerable coincidence, his father regularly played golf with the *Western Mail*'s Managing Director, Sir Robert J. Webber. So one day while playing golf, Richard Illingworth, using all his persuasive skills, was able to talk Sir Robert

One of Illingworth's earliest cartoons for the *Western Mail* published on 13 October 1921

into giving his son a part-time job in the *Western Mail's* lithographic department in Cardiff. Leslie Illingworth was thrilled with this opportunity, especially since he was still at school. At the *Western Mail*, he was primarily employed in the lithography department printing maps and doing drawings on stone. As he had made a good impression, the newspaper soon offered him the chance to draw both a regular sporting cartoon entitled *Dai Pepper* for the weekly *Football Express*, which was part of the *Western Mail*, as well as cartoons for its daily evening title, the *Evening Express*.

The *Western Mail* was in fact one of the first newspapers in Britain to carry regular political cartoons. These had been drawn since 1893 by the paper's chief cartoonist, Joseph Morewood Staniforth. Staniforth had also, since 1898, drawn cartoons every Sunday for the *News of the World*, which was owned by the same newspaper group as the *Western Mail*. Sir Robert Webber was so impressed with Illingworth's progress and talent as a cartoonist that he encouraged him to try his hand at political cartoons by deputising for Staniforth whenever he was away or unwell. Illingworth was thrilled and could not believe his luck. This is what he now wanted to do for a living more than anything else. As he later said:

> From the beginning I wanted to be a cartoonist. You're not self-wrapped-up if you're a cartoonist. You have to take attitudes about life.

Illingworth's rather morbid tribute to fellow cartoonist J M Staniforth published on 20 December 1921 in the *Western Mail*

A NATIONAL LOSS.

In 1920, Illingworth won yet another scholarship, this time to the Royal College of Art in London, where he received enormous encouragement from its principal, William Rothenstein. Illingworth was still able to fill in for Staniforth while studying at the Royal College. However, after six months at the College, Illingworth was informed that Staniforth, whose health had been in serious decline for some time, had died. The *Western Mail* had no hesitation in offering the 19-year-old Illingworth a full-time position, at the princely sum of £6 per week. Illingworth accepted this opportunity, describing it as "untold gold" and "tremendous". He returned immediately to Cardiff to take up his new post as a full-time political cartoonist. Illingworth realised it was time for him to get a sound grounding in political philosophy. He had up to now focused almost entirely on the artistic and gag side of cartooning. It was now, more than ever, important for him to understand the political scene if he was to succeed, as he later admitted:

> When I was young I read Marx and even Engels. I read everything I could. I was very interested in politics. Where I come from in Wales they are very political. It's near the coal area.

Leslie Illingworth at work in the 'Barn'. This was a large building acquired with Picketson Cottage. The upper level at one end was floored and partitioned off to form Leslie's studio.

Illingworth moved back in with his parents and set up his drawing board in a converted studio in his father's barn. From there he cycled and later drove in to Cardiff each day to the offices of the *Western Mail*. The newspaper was Conservative in its political outlook, which jarred with Illingworth's own left-wing views at the time. Although free to express his own political beliefs through his cartoons, he knew that, if he was to keep his job, he would have to follow the general editorial line of the newspaper. As he recollected:

> Nobody suggested ideas when I started on the *Western Mail*; I knew very well what the politics of the paper were, and I knew which side of my bread was buttered. The cartoonist must have a pragmatic approach.

Published in the *Western Mail* 14 January 1924 on the subject of Lloyd George's brief flirtation with the Labour Party.

In November 1923, while Illingworth was still at the *Western Mail*, Owen Aves, the Art Editor of the humorous weekly *Passing Show*, sent him a joke featuring pigs to illustrate. On seeing the result, Aves invited him to submit work by post. When Aves left *Passing Show* soon after and set up as an artists' agent, he shrewdly took on Illingworth and began to send down commissions for him to supply illustrations for the London market, in magazines such as *London Opinion, The Humorist, Pearson's, Strand, Nash's, Good Housekeeping, London Life, Tit-Bits, and Everybody's*. Illingworth's fee for illustrating a short story was a whopping 75 guineas. He later recalled, "I was a good artist, and I could make a lot of money." Later that same year he returned to London to study part-time at the Slade School of Art, while continuing to draw for the *Western Mail* and for Aves's agency.

Two examples of Illingworth's illustrative work, in this instance, for the *Passing Show*. Always beautifully and precisely drawn, Illingworth's style was heavily influenced by the magazine illustrator Steven Spurrier (1878–1961).

In May 1926, during the General Strike, the *Western Mail*'s print department refused to make the blocks for reproduction plates for Illingworth's cartoons. Illingworth felt no qualms about making them himself and was thus able to continue working for the paper. Not surprisingly, there were work colleagues and local miners' families critical of him for showing no solidarity with the miners' plight by continuing to work during the strike. "It was war, you know," Illingworth later said, "I was a blackleg." Despite this, Illingworth considered himself supportive of the miners and found the *Western Mail*'s uncompromising editorial stance in attacking the miners uncomfortable. He was certainly uneasy about defending the Welsh coal owners, but youth and a puckish sense of fun quieted any misgivings his conscience may have given him.

By late 1927, Illingworth, feeling the pressure of producing a daily cartoon and under the weather from overwork, decided he needed a break. He could now afford to do so as he was earning as much for his illustrative work as he was for his cartoons in the *Western Mail*. According to Sir Robert Webber, Illingworth was given a cheque and six months' leave of absence to tour the art schools of France and America. In France, he settled in Paris where the devalued franc meant he could rent a sizeable flat and resume his art education at the *Academy Julien*. From Paris, he regularly sent back magazine illustrations on the Imperial Airways aeroplanes to the London agency. Then, after completing his art course, he sailed from Liverpool on the Cunard liner *Alaunia* to New York, to work for three months as a political cartoonist for Hearst newspapers. William Randolph Hearst owned the British magazines *Good Housekeeping* and *Nash's*, to which Illingworth had been a regular contributor. He also drew for *Life*, then still the leading humorous magazine in the USA, which at the time was owned and edited by the famous American cartoonist, Charles Dana Gibson, illustrator and creator of the *Gibson Girl*. Illingworth then bought a car for the equivalent of £200 and for six months wandered his way around the United States until he reached San Francisco:

> I saw San Francisco before they had built the Golden Gate. In those days the roads after Chicago petered out into dust tracks. If you had a rainstorm you could not go on.

Remarkably, Illingworth was able to sell the car in San Francisco for a profit. He then decided to leave the United States and returned to Paris for a while before moving back to England and settling in St. Johns Wood, London, studying albeit periodically at the Slade School of Art. From there, he once again began to contribute cartoons to the *Western Mail*. While he had been away, J.C. Walker had been employed in his place on the paper, so Illingworth agreed to share the cartoon slot with him until Walker took on the job full-time towards the end of 1929. After another trip to the United States in 1930, Illingworth moved his increasingly prosperous freelance operation back to the studio in his father's barn at St. Athan. Throughout the 1930s he worked prodigiously, widening his remit to include advertisement illustration for clients such as Winsor and Newton, Kraft Cheese, Grey's Cigarettes, Symington's Soups, Eiffel Tower Lemonade and Wolsey Underwear. In 1937, *The Artist* described Illingworth as 'among the half dozen most eminent magazine artists of our day'.

On 27 May 1931, Illingworth's long association with *Punch* began when his first cartoon appeared in the magazine. However, the idea behind it, about a boy bursting a balloon-seller's balloons, was based on somebody else's joke. From thereon in he supplied *Punch* regularly with gag cartoons. However, the 'big cut', *Punch's* weekly political and social comment cartoon (two were published in each week's issue) was carried out by Sir Bernard Partridge and E H Shepard. When in 1937 the 70-year-old Partridge fell ill, Illingworth was invited to fill in for him. The 'big cut' was decided, as it had always been, by an editorial committee at the weekly Wednesday luncheon around the *Punch* 'Round Table'. At the lunch the editor, Sir Edmund Valpy Knox, along with the art editor

The Illingworth Family (left to right) Phyllis (sister), Leslie holding his nephew Richard, Vivian (brother), May (Vivian's wife), Helen (Mother) and Richard (Father).
This photograph was taken in the garden at the Illingworth family home, Picketston Cottage, St Athan, in the Vale of Glamorgan, Spring 1933.

and cartoonist Kenneth Bird (Fougasse), would discuss the form and content of the cartoon with representatives of the owners of *Punch*. Once they had come up with an idea it would be discussed with the cartoonist, who would also be at the lunch. The cartoonist would then be expected to take the idea back to the drawing board and put pen to paper. Years later, Illingworth remembered fondly that it was never as easy to complete his cartoon for *Punch* as it should have been:

> Very civilised it is. You sit there enjoying the conversation of some very nice people indeed. You drink some very nice wine and some brandy, and come away feeling very good indeed. It's not always possible to start drawing afterwards.

The style of *Punch*'s political cartoons of this period was still in the Tenniel 'Grand Manner' of the previous century. They were expected to be noble and oracular; the very essence of Victorian gentility. Compared with Illingworth's later work for the *Daily Mail*, his cartoons for *Punch*, although always beautifully and meticulously drawn with exquisite detail and line, lacked bite or any semblance of wit. As Partridge's health continued to decline, Illingworth contributed an ever-increasing number of 'big cuts'. When war broke out in September 1939, Partridge moved out of London and Illingworth went on to share the twice-weekly task as junior partner to E H Shepard. Partridge continued to contribute occasionally to *Punch*, where he was still treated with extreme deference, having worked there since 1891. Illingworth remembered being customarily bundled down the back stairs whenever Partridge came into the building. By the time Partridge died in 1945, Illingworth was considered better than Shepard and promoted to lead cartoonist. He continued to draw the 'big cut' until his retirement from *Punch* in 1968.

In 1936, with an increasing amount of his work continuing to come in from London, Illingworth decided it would make more sense for him to move back there. Browsing through the newspapers, he saw an advertisement in *The Times* for a flat to let at 53 Queensborough Terrace, Bayswater. Having answered the advertisement, Illingworth met the owner of the flat, Enid Ratcliff, who agreed to take him on as a tenant for 37s 6d a week. It was the beginning of a relationship that would last a lifetime.

After war had been declared on Germany in September 1939, Illingworth found to his cost that the illustration market had dried up as publishers and advertisers cut back. Despite the lack of work, Illingworth also felt an urgent need to express his antipathy towards the Nazis and knew the best way to do that was through cartooning. With the apparent success of his work in *Punch*, one imagines that Illingworth would not have found it too difficult to find a position on either a national or a provincial newspaper. Political cartoons were now very much in fashion. Newspapers that had never carried them now did so. For example, Philip Zec at the *Daily Mirror*, who had previously been an illustrator and had never drawn a political cartoon before, was employed as the paper's first political cartoonist. Many of the provincial newspapers, which no longer carried sports cartoons because of the war, successfully employed their sports cartoonist to draw political cartoons instead. This happened most successfully in the case of George Butterworth at the *Daily Dispatch*, Arthur Potts at the *Bristol Evening World* and John Furnival at the *Lancashire Evening Post*.

In February 1938, Percy Fearon, better known under his pseudonym 'Poy', had retired from the *Daily Mail* after a long and successful career. He had been Lord Northcliffe's favourite cartoonist. At the time the *Daily Mail* had the fourth largest circulation of any national daily behind the *Daily Express, Daily Herald* and the *Daily Mirror*. Despite this, the paper appeared to be in no particular hurry to find a successor although, as already mentioned, they had appointed that year Illingworth's early school friend Ronald Niebour as an illustrator. When war broke out, the paper realised it needed a political cartoonist, like its competitors, to help raise the morale of its readership. Niebour was immediately given a regular slot to draw a pocket cartoon mocking the enemy. In October 1939, the *Daily Mail* advertised for a political cartoonist. When Illingworth's friend and fellow cartoonist, Clive Uptton, was turned down by the *Daily Mail* through lack of experience as a political cartoonist, he decided to apply himself. Illingworth, however, was concerned that his somewhat anodyne work for *Punch* would work against him, as he later recalled:

> I couldn't tell them I was Illingworth because they would know me, I was doing fuddy-duddy drawings for *Punch* and I wouldn't have got the job.

So Illingworth contrived to have a couple of cartoons inserted in a big batch of 'unknowns' submitted by his agent, Owen Aves, most of them the work of younger, less experienced, artists. He signed his two cartoons "MacGregor" (his mother's maiden name) and drew them in a much simpler style than he had used for *Punch* and his illustration work. As Illingworth hoped, they caught the eye of the deputy editor of the *Daily Mail*, Gordon Beckles. However, unbeknown to Illingworth, Beckles was suspicious, as he recognised his style in the cartoons. Beckles then invited the so-called Mr. MacGregor to call round for an interview. When Illingworth arrived at the deputy editor's door, Beckles, a very tall man, greeted him:

> "Mr. MacGregor?" he asked.
> "Ye-es," said Illingworth, nervously

'Alias Mr. MacGregor' Illingworth at the start of his career at the *Daily Mail*

> "You are sure," said the editor accusingly, "your name is not Illingworth?"
> Illingworth blanched and glanced fearfully up: "Yes sir, it's Illingworth, sir, I'm very sorry."

Illingworth, despite his worst fears and to his great surprise, was offered the job there and then at a salary of £1,500 a year, which rose to £2,000 after the first three months. At the age of 37, he was now working for a leading national newspaper and competing with the greatest political cartoonists in the land, such as Sidney Strube at the *Daily Express*, David Low at the *Evening Standard*, George Whitelaw on the *Daily Herald* and Victor Weisz (Vicky) on the *News Chronicle*. He was also, much to his relief, working in a reserved occupation, which meant it was unlikely that he would be conscripted, as his brother had just been at the age of 40. Illingworth admitted later with a fair degree of candour that he had also joined the *Daily Mail* "for nothing but cowardly reasons – I didn't want to go into the Army." He feared that, as in the First World War, as a soldier he would be nothing more than 'cannon fodder'. Instead he had got that safe 'desk job', later stating, "thank God I succeeded."

The *Daily Mail*, like the *Western Mail*, was a firmly Conservative newspaper. Illingworth had few qualms over this. Earning good money throughout the 1930s had changed his political outlook and he was now firmly in the Tory camp. In any case, with Britain at war, party politics was largely irrelevant. Illingworth knew exactly on whom to focus his attentions. As he later recalled:

> It was absolutely easy – there's no doubt about it. We were against Hitler, against Mussolini, against Stalin to start with and then for him immediately as soon as he came in.

Unlike many of the cartoonists working on other newspapers, Illingworth had the advantage of having seen the Nazi leaders in the flesh. In the 1930s he had visited Garmisch, the winter sports centre near Munich, and had seen most of them close up. He later recounted:

> Hitler, in particular, seemed peculiarly repulsive, with his pasty, flabby face and a certain effeminacy about his movements. The only one for whom I did not feel an instinctive dislike was Goebbels; perhaps it was because his features, though ugly enough, revealed a redeeming sense of humour – though it has since turned out to be a sardonic one.

Illingworth's first cartoon for the *Daily Mail* (page 31) – an attack on Government bureaucracy – appeared on Monday 30 October 1939. From then on, he produced three to four cartoons a week while continuing to draw the weekly cartoon for *Punch*. He even found time to continue his book illustration work in addition to wartime propaganda drawings for the Ministry of Health and Ministry of Information. His association with the *Daily Mail* was to last 30 years and span nine editorships. The demands of the daily newspaper deadlines brought a new simplicity of style and forcefulness to his work, which was radically different from the dull, benign but intricate full-page drawings he was producing for *Punch*. The cartoons he was now drawing for the *Daily Mail* were similar in style to the ones he had previously produced for the *Western Mail*, but the execution of his line was now bolder and more self-assured. However, with the pressures of meeting the deadline on a daily cartoon, with time at a premium, Illingworth was left rarely satisfied with his finished drawing. From a purely technical point of view he much preferred his work for *Punch*, for which he had a week to complete. Sometimes, as an expression of private dissatisfaction with a cartoon, Illingworth would simply leave off his signature. Once the drawing had been handed to the editor he never wanted to see the published version. As fellow cartoonist Keith Mackenzie later observed:

> By a curious quirk, once the drawing is out of his hands he never wants to see it in print and cannot bear to open the paper with his drawing in it.

Although the ideas for Illingworth's *Punch* cartoons were decided by a weekly committee, the procedure at the *Daily Mail* was different. As a staff cartoonist, Illingworth would come up with three or four ideas for a cartoon to show his editor, who would then choose the one he considered the best or the most appropriate. It would appear that the editor would often choose the subject matter for the cartoons as they were sometimes used to illustrate articles in the paper and as the majority of Illingworth's cartoons relate to articles in the paper itself this would suggest that the cartoonist was often told which story to cover. The difference was that the ideas for the *Daily Mail* unlike *Punch* were entirely Illingworth's own, as he freely admitted:

> I've never been told what to do. Never, never, never. The best editor is a man that will look at your roughs and say "Oh, wonderful! Good! That's the one I want".

Illingworth loved his studio at the *Daily Mail*, a small private office on the fourth floor of Northcliffe House on the corner of Whitefriars Street and Tudor Street, close to London's Fleet Street. Unlike David Low and Carl Giles, who preferred to work away from the newspaper so as not to be interfered with or disturbed as they produced their work, Illingworth revelled in a busy workplace. He loved the excitement of a newspaper office, the thrill of being at the centre of things. A colleague thought it kept him "fresh and young, fit and happy". His room, according to Wally Fawkes, was always "stuffed with people" chattering away while Illingworth quite happily got on with his drawing amongst all the commotion. There were times when he needed his own space and solitude, and for this he rented a special garret room in Temple Chambers, equidistant from *Punch* and Northcliffe House, for the unhurried execution of his weekly *Punch* cartoon.

Despite the pressure of deadlines, Illingworth had immense patience. Pat Murphy, a colleague at the *Daily Mail*, recalled on one occasion how Illingworth had almost completed a scraperboard drawing for *Punch* with a theme based on Shelley's poem 'The Cloud' and illustrating the line 'like a swarm of golden bees...' when all of a sudden disaster struck. Having intricately drawn about 650 bees with their four wings and six legs and a dense complicated countryside background, a gust of wind whipped the drawing off his easel and out of his office window. He walked over to the balustrade and peered down, muttering: "I bet it goes face down." It not only went face down but a *Daily Mail* van drove over it, destroying the six or seven hours' work Illingworth had spent on the nearly finished drawing. According to Murphy, "Leslie pulled out another huge board from his quiver of them and, saying 'Oh! Aye, start all over again', Illingworth began to do exactly that." He was simply unflappable.

Illingworth manning an ack-ack gun

Illingworth's natural good nature, patience and generosity to colleagues and friends were especially extended to younger aspiring cartoonists, who all referred to him as Uncle Leslie. When a young and exasperated Bernard Cookson went to see him for some advice on how to deal with an editor who did not appreciate his ideas for a cartoon that morning, Illingworth told him to "bend with the wind boyo! Bend with the wind." Cookson believed this guidance on how to deal with difficult editors helped him throughout his career. Everyone who met Illingworth found him amiable. According to Wally Fawkes he had "huge magnetism" and always offered great encouragement to budding cartoonists. Another colleague on the *Daily Mail*, Colin Reid, found Illingworth had such an enormous zest for living that made being with him uplifting. Malcolm Muggeridge found him to be "a very loveable, original, gifted human being".

During the Blitz, Illingworth found himself putting out incendiaries on the roof of the *Daily Mail*'s offices in Fleet Street. After volunteering to join the Local Defence Volunteers (later the Home Guard) during 1940, he found himself two years later serving as a night time gunner with the Home Guard Battery Z (a rocket battery) in an anti-aircraft unit in Hyde Park. One evening, Illingworth's old school friend Glyn Daniel, then an R.A.F. Intelligence Officer who would later go on to become a Cambridge professor of Welsh archaeology and find fame on the TV programme "Going for a Song", met up with Illingworth while on duty at his anti-aircraft unit. They both looked towards the City of London which that evening was in flames and the distant crunching noise of exploding German bombs could be heard. In response, Illingworth turned to Daniel and said: "They won't win, they can't win. It's all so evil and evil can't win."

Illingworth acquired a large flat in Knightsbridge for him and Enid (by now his housekeeper) to live in. This part of West London was relatively safe from bombing as the Luftwaffe generally concentrated on London's East End and the docks. He also allowed Czech Jewish refugees to stay there. These included the political cartoonist Stephen Roth, who was then drawing sporting cartoons for the *Daily Mail* and political ones for the *Sunday Pictorial*. For weekend relaxation, Illingworth took a cottage in Surrey, where he kept a number of farm animals. Enid soon joined him and within a year they moved in to a larger property in Horley on the Surrey/Sussex border, which Enid had originally bought as a home for evacuee children from London with an inheritance from her father.

Illingworth very quickly developed a strong following amongst readers of the paper. When exhibitions of his original cartoons were held in department stores such as Kendal Milne & Co, Manchester, in 1940, and Lewis's Stores, Glasgow in 1943, they proved to be immensely popular with the general public. In 1941, the *Daily Mail* boasted that figures of Illingworth's creation had become "the political furniture of our minds. In momentous times like these such artists gain a secure position with posterity. Their work conveys at a glance more than later generations can learn from columns of print."

As the war continued, Illingworth also became well known in North America, where an international version of the *Daily Mail* had become available. On 17 April 1944, for instance, *Newsweek* referred to Illingworth as "one of Britain's best-known cartoonists – perhaps second only to the world-famous David Low. The tremendous circulation of the *Daily Mail* gave Illingworth a British-American audience rivalling the estimated 20, 000,000 of Low."

Illingworth's working day at the *Daily Mail* changed little over the 30 years he held his position there. On a typical day, he would listen to the early morning news on the radio as soon as he got out of bed and then review all the morning national dailies over breakfast. Illingworth's nephew, Julian Lewis, remembers staying with him, where he would cook breakfast while 'Uncle Leslie was soaking in the bath reading *The Times* in order to get an idea for that day's cartoon'. By the time he arrived in Fleet Street several promising ideas would be taking shape in his mind. According to cartoonist Charles Grave, if you asked Illingworth how he worked he would tell you, "He reads the newspapers and creates concrete symbols of the news. His trouble, he says, is that he doesn't think in words, and he just can't do snappy captions." Illingworth, with several ideas in mind, would first grab a pencil and just doodle and in this way would quickly come up with rough compositions:

> I do little doodles of the ideas I get. Doodles suggest something else.
> It's a continuing process, you do another little doodle.

Wally Fawkes believed that what was so remarkable about Illingworth's roughs was that they were so "full of vigour" and that his completed drawing would actually lose a certain amount of that 'vigour'. Before lunch, Illingworth would present three or four of these roughs to his editor, who would decide which one to go with and then suggest the appropriate shape of the cartoon for that day's page layout. After lunch the real work would begin. He would redraw the roughly pencilled design on a virgin sheet of board when the situation, likeness and background would then be rapidly drawn in with a fine pen, strengthened by brush, chalk, mechanical tint or wash. Fellow cartoonist Bill Hewison believed Illingworth had a "faultless pen and ink technique". According to

Hewison it was a technique that was "essentially naturalistic yet masterly in its variety of textures, arrangement of tones, and subtle atmospheric perspective. It is hardly cartooning."

Illingworth was, surprisingly, the only cartoonist to occasionally use scraperboard for his cartoons. Its use when required would dramatise the effect of light and dark within a composition. Illingworth used scratchboard, a chalk surface drawing paper and a fine pointed tool or a penknife to delicately etch his lines out of the inky shadows in the manner of a wood engraving. The effect, according to John Geipel in his short history of graphic comedy and satire, was that by juxtaposing deftly wrought detail with areas of thunderous black, Illingworth achieved a richness and authority that distinguished his work from all his contemporaries.

Illingworth saw everything in visual terms and to him cartoons were simply pictorial analogies of an actual situation. This meant that the main advantage of cartoons over newspaper articles was that, as visual images, they received immediate recognition from the reader and could be more quickly understood and appreciated by them:

> I think cartooning can communicate to all the readers of the newspaper. I think that they can apprehend the cartoon quicker than any editorial. People do not need words; like animals, they are aware of things. If it comes to the surface, it comes as a visual impression. Literary people may think with words, but I am very suspicious of it. Words are a late thing. Basic communication does not need words. Feelings do not need words. Animals communicate with each other.

Although he was easily able to express himself in visual terms, Illingworth found it difficult to do so verbally. Not surprisingly, he avoided speaking in public. Once he complained bitterly about an editor who forced him and two competing cartoonists to talk about their ideas for that day's drawing in full conference before choosing which of them got the job. As Illingworth recalled:

> I hate to speak in public. I am not at ease with words. I forget the names and I am a man who thinks with pictures not words and so to sit among a gaggle of people who know how to express themselves and expect me to speak. It was awful.

Unlike most cartoonists, Illingworth did not rely on photographic references, preferring to draw things he knew well from memory. He believed, like all good draughtsmen, that it was important to draw things accurately whether, for example, it was an expression, a facial feature, a steamroller or a windmill. According to Illingworth:

> You should represent the absolute truth even if you distort it. I want the barn to stay up and the motorbike to move.

It took approximately four hours to finish his daily drawing, after corrections and deletions had been done with either white ink (the forerunner of Tippex) or razor blade. Around the 7.30pm deadline for the *Daily Mail*'s Scottish edition, the drawing would be sent down to the Process Department to produce the line block ready for printing. Then every Thursday night, having completed his daily cartoon, he would settle down in his small room in Temple Chambers to devote time and care to his *Punch* cartoon. It was thought out before supper, pencilled in before retiring and executed as dawn crept up behind the dominant silhouette of St Paul's, which filled the window. Indeed such was his devotion to his *Punch* work that he sometimes finished his weekly cartoon in the *Daily Mail*'s office. At times, he struggled to complete his workload and was often being chased for the finished drawing by editor and agent alike. He would also try to delay the cartoon's departure, according to his nephew Richard, by soft-soaping the editor's secretary whenever he was being chased because the deadline for his cartoon had passed. Left to him, Illingworth would go on working away on his cartoon indefinitely and sometimes, according to one of the editors he worked under, "it had to be snatched from him by cunning or brute force." On one occasion, his agent burst into his office and demanded he produce the work immediately as it was well overdue. Illingworth turned to him and said:

> I'll tell you what I'll do. I'll compromise. I'll say I will and then I won't.

In February 1944, Illingworth got the sad news that his only brother, Lieutenant-Colonel Vivian Illingworth, had died of leukaemia while on active service in Naples. An example of Illingworth's enormous generosity was that he made sure that Vivian's son, Richard, had a private school education by paying his fees throughout his time at Bedales Public School in Hampshire.

After entering Hitler's Berlin bunker, a British fusilier discovered this cartoon published in the *Daily Mail* on 29 March 1944. It still bore a label to show it had been filed away by Joseph Goebbels.

At the end of the war Illingworth was amazed to find that some of his cartoons, cut out from the pages of the *Daily Mail*, had been found in a safe in Hitler's bunker. It was also discovered that his name had been put on a Nazi hit list of those who were to be executed should the Germans have succeeded in invading Britain in 1940. Illingworth considered it something of a badge of honour to have upset the Nazi hierarchy to the extent that they kept cuttings of his cartoons, as well as wanting him liquidated.

Illingworth in his office with fellow *Daily Mail* cartoonist Roland Neibour 'Neb'

In 1946, he gave up his book and commercial work to concentrate on his cartoons for the *Daily Mail* and *Punch*. Illingworth also decided he had had enough of urban life and that year found exactly what he wanted – Silverdale, an early Victorian farmhouse outside Robertsbridge, East Sussex which he bought for £5,000.

As already mentioned, Illingworth was politically at home on the *Daily Mail* and in complete accord with the editorial column which he often illustrated. His cartoons therefore naturally found favour with the majority of the paper's readership. He later said:

> I think you must be at one with the people you are drawing for. I am lower middle class and I was drawing for lower middle class people and it is a good thing because I was in touch with them.

Wally Fawkes, his successor at the *Daily Mail*, thought that Illingworth was a 'county conservative' who believed that the Monarchy and the upper class elite that then made up the Conservative Party at Westminster were born to run the country. It was to him the natural order of things. Fawkes, who produced the *Flook* strip in the *Daily Mail*, remembered trying to defend the Labour leaders to Illingworth, who would have nothing of it, as he believed that, because they did not have the right accents, they were not the Country's natural born leaders.

Illingworth was thus happy to preach to the converted. By doing so his cartoons were not, contentious, unsurprisingly. He admitted that he never wanted to upset anyone, especially the readers. This today would be considered something of a disadvantage to a political cartoonist. Often the best cartoons are those that lead to the reader sitting up and taking note or, even better, making him or her rage with fury or indignation. Unlike Illingworth, David Low held political views that were diametrically opposed to those of the paper he worked for. This meant that his cartoons made a much bigger impact on the paper's readers. There were often lively debates in the readers' section of the *Evening Standard* after Low had drawn a cartoon attacking one sacred cow or another. Low was famously allowed to stretch the boundaries on issues that were then considered either taboo or in very poor taste. This would have been impossible in any case for cartoonists like Illingworth, whose editor would always have had the final say. Low worked away from the newspaper in his own studio and so produced what he wanted. The paper would, of course, have the right to refuse publication, but rarely did. But unlike those on the Left, such as Low and Vicky, Illingworth did not want to change the world, just to comment on it. This was a natural line for him to follow, because to him cartoons neither altered people's opinions nor their political allegiances.

A caricature of Illingworth by trumpeter and bandleader, Humphrey Lyttelton. Lyttelton who drew under the pseudonym 'Humph', had been employed by the *Daily Mail* in 1949 to draw column-breakers, which were humorous or decorative cartoons that were inserted in the text. He also, until 1953, wrote the story-line for Wally Fawkes's 'Flook' cartoon.

Cartoonists therefore did not, according to Illingworth, have a large influence on the public, as they were simply to him just 'a little froth on the surface of politics'. Illingworth, although in sympathy with the readers of the *Daily Mail*, believed that the paper's readership still made up a spectrum of different views and beliefs and, in attempting to cater to all, the cartoon could lose any chance of impacting itself on the reader. According to Illingworth:

> If a cartoon is for everybody, you cannot do anything except a bland thing.

Illingworth felt that those cartoonists who drew for a smaller audience – on a provincial or evening paper, for example – had more chance of making a greater impression on the reader:

> When you draw for a national daily, you draw for such a large crowd that you cannot do it properly. But once you have a small thing – like Low had in the *Evening Standard* – a restricted audience, you can be all the more powerful. Low drew for the people at Westminster and I think he did have an effect on them.

Although a Conservative, Illingworth held no strong ideological beliefs and had a native distrust of zealots of all political backgrounds. To him politics was a pragmatic thing. It was the art of the possible and was all about making life better for the man in the street. He thought that any fervent political ideology, when put into practice, would always end in ruining lives not bettering them. As he once explained:

> There has been more unhappiness in the world caused by people who supported communism or fascism. And they killed and tortured and it's a tragedy to find people that believed in these things so much that they should forget man. I believe in a local politics, which has to do with drains, the cost of food and that sort of thing. But once you get into the romantic sort of politics you always start killing in the end, and it's bad, bad. I am against that. I was not when I was young. I used to think that some people had money, some had little and they starved and that it was wrong. I gave up thinking so when I was 25 or so.

Artist John Minton, Wally Fawkes 'Trog' and Illingworth

Illingworth was therefore poles apart from the likes of Vicky and Low, whose political convictions were an anathema to him. He even went as far to say of Vicky: "He's sincere. He's zealous, yes. And that's why he's an utter clot. I'm not a zealot in any way at all." Despite his political zeal, Illingworth did think that Low was still the greatest cartoonist of the Twentieth Century. Sadly, Illingworth was always under the impression that Low disliked him, which most likely was because of their divergent political beliefs.

Illingworth was a born cynic and certainly did not take seriously those on the Left who believed it was possible to create a utopian New Jerusalem. For the sake of perspective, he preferred to see things from a distance, viewing the political scene with the dispassionate expertise of a mechanic dismantling an engine. Cartoonist Bernard Hollowood noted how Illingworth lacked passionate involvement. The advantage of taking such a detached view was that it allowed him to avoid resenting those he ridiculed: as David Low once said of malice, it all too frequently clouds the mind.

After the war, Illingworth was able to focus his attention on Labour's first majority Government, which lasted from July 1945 until October 1951. He thought it a travesty that the British electorate had rejected Churchill, the man who had won the war. The Labour leaders were portrayed as hapless political minnows by comparison with Churchill, who were incapable of

CURIOUSER AND CURIOUSER
This cartoon published on 3 February 1961 was in regard to the disastrous merger between Charles Clore's and Jack Cotton's property companies. Remarkably, Macmillan publishers, who then owned the copyright to Sir John Tenniel's work, sent Illingworth a 'gentle rebuke and a bill for five guineas' for breach of copyright. It appears a coincidence that the Prime Minister Harold Macmillan actually appears in the cartoon.

rebuilding post-war Britain. To Illingworth it was Labour that was responsible for all of Britain's ills, e.g. the privations of shortages and rationing. The diminutive Prime Minister, Clement Attlee, and his cohorts Morrison, Cripps, Dalton and especially the inept Shinwell, were ridiculed mercilessly day after day in his cartoons in the *Daily Mail*. To Illingworth the Welsh firebrand Aneuran Bevan, came in for special attention after referring to the Conservatives as 'lower than vermin'. Despite this, Bevan's wife, Jennie Lee, requested an original cartoon she had seen in the *Daily Mail* of Bevan with no clothes on. On receiving the original from Illingworth she wrote back to him stating that it was exactly like him.

When Churchill and the Conservatives returned to power in 1951, Illingworth divided his attention between the divisions in the Labour Opposition and the Cold War. When Labour regained power in 1964, Harold Wilson became the central focus of Illingworth's ridicule, closely followed by Foreign Secretary George Brown. Illingworth's faith in the eventual triumph of goodness and right, as had occurred at the end of the war, began to falter as he drew with sadness and gloom post-war events first in Korea, then Hungary, Africa, Czechoslovakia and finally Vietnam. Of such things, he was often heard to say:

> It's all wrong boyo. It's all wrong. We're all going to hell!

It was not until the *Punch* editorship of Malcolm Muggeridge in 1953 that Illingworth found his most inspiring and incisive direction at *Punch*. Muggeridge recalled that since Illingworth "did not have a strongly political mind, a whole series of suggestions could be put to him without him reacting strongly." As a result, this collaboration produced the cartoonist's most powerful and best-remembered drawing, which appeared in *Punch* on 3 February 1954. This was his cartoon of an ageing Winston Churchill entitled 'Man Goeth Forth unto his Work and his Labour until the Evening', suggesting that it was time he retired as Prime Minister. This caused widespread indignation among Conservative publicists and politicians and caused a row between the editor and proprietors of *Punch*. This cartoon can be seen in *Churchill in Caricature* (PCS, 2005). Churchill was himself bitterly hurt by the cartoon: "Yes, there's malice in it. Look at my hands - I have beautiful hands. *Punch* goes everywhere. I shall have to retire if this sort of thing goes on." Churchill's doctor, Lord Moran, was also shocked by what he considered a vicious caricature of the Prime Minister:

> There was something un-English in this savage attack on his [Churchill] failing powers. The eyes were dull and lifeless. There was no tone in the flaccid muscles; the jowl sagged. It was the expressionless mask of extreme old age.

It must have pained Illingworth to have to draw it because he practically hero-worshipped Churchill. Worse still, Churchill had been a constant admirer of Illingworth's work having written to him on several occasions congratulating him and asking for the original cartoon. It was rumoured that Muggeridge soon became well known in Churchill circles as 'Buggeridge'. Angry letters poured in to *Punch*'s offices. One of these letters of complaint was from Christopher Soames, in defence of his father-in-law. As Churchill later recalled: "Christopher wrote to that awful fellow, Muggeridge. He knows him, lives in his neighbourhood. Muggeridge wrote back saying that he was a journalist. If he held opinions, he must express them; said that he was one of my greatest admirers, but that I was no longer up to the job." Despite this episode, Illingworth enjoyed working under Muggeridge's editorship. As he later recalled:

> He was a very exciting and witty editor. I sat on his right side at the famous *Punch* table. On my right sat Sir John Betjeman; bless them they were very kind to me. I was conscious that I was a monumental bore, so I used to concentrate on the claret and keep as quiet as a cabbage.

Life imitating art – a caricaturist's dream

Illingworth's appearance might have been a better subject for caricature than the majority of those he actually included in his cartoons. He was of medium height, with a stocky build, a very large rugged face with pink cheeks, almost no neck and an underslung jaw. In his youth he had had bright red hair, which in later adulthood had turned white, with increasingly large bushy eyebrows spread above his steely bluish grey eyes. Basil Boothroyd, assistant editor of *Punch* in the 1950s, described Illingworth as having "the lineaments of an immensely genial monkey, with eyebrows like hedges and a radiant prognathous grin." Illingworth believed his lack of neck was a genetic thing:

> I have no neck. All the Illingworths have no necks. When I visited Mexico in the 1950s I came across a local businessman with the same name – and he had no neck, just like me.

As a consequence of his physical appearance Illingworth, having a very low opinion of himself, thought he was ugly, although there was never a shortage of female admirers. When a journalist once arrived to interview him for an article, Illingworth said in all frankness and modesty: "How nice of you to make me a celebrity. I'd better warn you that I'm not very pretty." Although Malcolm Muggeridge considered Illingworth's appearance and manner to be rough, he thought it absurd that, like George Orwell, Illingworth considered himself to be ugly. However, according to his friend Glyn Daniel, Illingworth enjoyed drawing himself in an exaggerated way as a hairy Neanderthal: "He enjoyed laughing at himself as he laughed at the world."

In 1956, the then *Daily Mail* editor decided he wanted a more modern style of cartoon in the paper. Illingworth found, somewhat to his annoyance, that two other cartoonists were employed by the editor to alternate alongside him. They were John Musgrave Wood (Emmwood) and George Chrystal (Chrys). As a consequence, Illingworth's weekly output was reduced to two cartoons. It seemed no coincidence that the editor, himself a Yorkshireman, had employed another in Emmwood.

Apart from completing his usual quota of cartoons, Illingworth made police court drawings for the paper. He also drew wanted men by Scotland Yard, including a projection of how the Great Train Robber, Bruce Reynolds, might look after plastic surgery.

Illingworth's recreations might have been described as the acquisition of homes and the entertainment of friends. He bought one of the first flats put up for sale in the Barbican in the 1960s and allowed friends to use it on the many occasions he was not there. At Fleet Street haunts such as El Vino and the Mucky Duck, Illingworth would often be found surrounded by colleagues and acquaintances, many of whom knew that their most difficult task lay in trying to settle their share of the bill before he did. Glyn Daniel was amazed by Illingworth's generosity to others:

> There is a curious English phrase 'generous to a fault' and I never quite knew what it meant until I knew Leslie. He gave of his time, money and resources with almost prodigal generosity. It was a curious contrast in his character that while he always wanted his friends and his family to have things he himself seemed to care little for the material possessions of this world in his own life.

In 1965, Illingworth was given a Special Award for Distinguished Services to Cartooning at the Dorchester Hotel by the Prime Minster Harold Wilson, the guest of honour. It must have been an awkward moment for Illingworth, whose cartoons had derided Wilson and the Labour Party for years.

By the late 1960s, Illingworth had become the longest serving cartoonist in Fleet Street. His wartime counterparts were either dead, such as Low, Strube and Vicky (who committed suicide in 1965) – or in retirement, such as Zec and Butterworth. When a journalist asked Illingworth how he had kept going for so long, he rather tongue-in-cheek replied:

> Ah my boy, I hide behind the door and when the editor comes in looking for someone to sack he doesn't see me.

Towards the end of 1969, at the age of 67, Illingworth finally decided to retire after precisely 30 years at the *Daily Mail*. According to Wally Fawkes he was happy to do so, having survived nine different editors. He was by now, in any case, fed up with the political scene and, rather astonishingly, believed that the British public was getting tired of international politics. More significantly, Illingworth also knew that as cartoonists aged their work began to deteriorate. This was normally as a result of worsening eyesight, ill heath or simply being burnt out after decades of

'It's a cartoonists' rally'

Daily Mirror
31 May 1968
Stanley Franklin's cartoon featuring Illingworth amongst many other cartoonists of the day. *They are left to right*, Keith Waite, Raymond Jackson 'JAK', Franklin himself, Gerald Scarfe , Michael Cummings, Osbert Lancaster, and (standing) Leslie Illingworth.

drawing daily cartoons. Illingworth wanted to go before he was pushed and to avoid the humiliation of being fired. According to Illingworth one is at one's best as a cartoonist until "up to 50–55. After that you go down the other side of the hump."

Illingworth had been forewarned. He had seen what had happened to those contemporaries of his who had gone on too long. For instance, Sidney Strube was sacked on his birthday after 36 years on the *Daily Express*. Michael Cummings, Strube's successor, said that he had become "stale and repetitive". Being sacked broke Strube's heart and he only lived a further eight years, dying in March 1956. Carl Giles was also fired after his work had declined following a long and illustrious career at the *Daily Express*. David Low, by the late 1950s, was suffering from emphysema after a lifetime of smoking. This clearly affected his work, although at times he could still produce the occasional brilliant cartoon as he done so regularly in the past. By 1962, his work had become embarrassingly bad and the editor of The *Guardian*, Alistair Hetherington, did his utmost to get rid of Low and replace him full-time with Bill Papas, who was sharing the cartoon slot with him. Before he was able to do so, Low's health deteriorated to such an extent that he was hospitalised, with his last cartoon appearing in The *Guardian* on 30 April 1963. He died five months later on 19 September. Illingworth watched the tragedy take place and believed that Low also suffered at the end because his dream of a socialist paradise failed to materialise. Low became disillusioned by firstly the obstinacy of the trade unions, and secondly by the fact that the Labour Party could not adapt to a society, caught in the consumer boom of the later 1950s, that simply wanted to better itself. According to Illingworth:

> Even old Low you know in the end wasn't very good. Mind, events defeated him. All the things he was advocating came to pass and he saw how horrid it was and he didn't know what he could do.

In June 1968, Illingworth met President Lyndon Johnson at the White House. "He's an agreeable man – fitted my cartoons exactly" Illingworth said afterwards. Whilst in Washington, Illingworth also attended the American Cartoonists Association's convention. Of the American cartoonists he met, illingworth said: "Apart from my Welsh accent they were most impressed by my eyebrows."

Before he left the *Daily Mail*, Illingworth lined up Wally Fawkes to replace him. Fawkes had already been drawing political cartoons for several months for the paper alongside Illingworth, as Chrys had left. Lord Rothermere, however, had other ideas. He thought Gerald Scarfe would be more fashionable and so employed him instead as Illingworth's replacement. After a short stint, Scarfe, who has always been more of a caricaturist concentrating on creating grotesque images of politicians than those one would expect from a political cartoonist, was dropped, and Wally Fawkes reinstated. Despite leaving the *Daily Mail*, Illingworth lived on as 'Organ Morgan', the Welsh farmer in Fawkes' *Flook* strip, which had been going since April 1949.

Illingworth in retirement, tending cattle at Silverdale.

In October 1970, an exhibition of Illingworth's work was held at the Boston Public Library in the United States, organised by a young American cartoon historian and biographer of James Gillray, by the name of Draper Hill. Hill said at the official opening that Illingworth was "simply the finest draughtsman of our time to have devoted himself to editorial caricature."

Illingworth retired happily to Silverdale, which now saw the growth of his other great love, farming. He had over the years visited neighbouring farms to watch how farm workers tended to their livestock. He expanded his farm at every opportunity. Every time a parcel of land adjoining Silverdale came up for sale he would purchase it, and he ended up with over 30 acres. As the farm grew, Enid would use a "great big handbell", given to Illingworth by the journalist Henry Fairlie, in order to summon him when he was at work in some remote corner of his farm should someone arrive at his door to see him or want him on the phone.

Illingworth later said that if he had not become a cartoonist he would have liked to have been an animal painter like Landseer, or an animal illustrator like Warwick Reynolds. He loved being down in East Sussex because other cartoonists who lived nearby often visited him. For instance, Francis Smith 'Smilby', who drew for *Playboy*, lived at Trumpetts Farm near Hurstmonceux; Alex Graham, who drew Fred Basset, lived at Ticehurst and Wally Fawkes had a house in Hastings.

However, Illingworth, whose hospitality, as already mentioned,was legendary, kept up the same level of entertaining as he had done before retiring. Those Fleet Street sops who had earlier taken advantage of his generosity still continued to do so, and the upkeep of his farm, a Georgian terrace house in Dulwich and a Barbican flat for his visits to London meant that by 1973 he found himself not only short of money but also being chased by the taxman for back taxes. Remarkably, the pursuance by the taxman led to Illingworth fleeing to France. He answered an advert for a gardener for a French villa. The French couple that had agreed to employ Illingworth were amazed to see him

Enid Ratcliff and Illingworth

turn up at their home in his Bentley along with Enid, his housekeeper. The problem was that Illingworth was soon homesick and found the villa particularly cold in the winter months. According to Illingworth's nephew, the villa was not really suitable for occupation in the winter. A cousin of Illingworth's agreed to bail him out with a loan so that he could pay his back taxes. One of the effects of this was that he had to start working again in order to pay back the loan.

At first, Illingworth was given the opportunity to stand in for the Australian Paul Rigby on the *Sun* for a month between December 1973 and January 1974. Upon his return, Rigby decided to give up his regular weekly cartoon for *The News of the World* as it was proving too much of a burden alongside drawing daily cartoons for the *Sun*. So he recommended Illingworth, who as a result got the job. His first cartoon appeared in the *News of the World* on 17 February 1974. Coincidentally, J M Staniforth, Illingworth's predecessor at the *Western Mail*, had also drawn cartoons for many years for the *News of the World* at the turn of the century. Illingworth, of course, now only had the one cartoon to do, which was regularly drawn on a Thursday. "Messing about with farming", as he called it, came to an abrupt halt while he digested every national newspaper daily for a clue to the political topic of the week. He would then take to the sunny wing of his farmhouse, perch himself on his elegant Victorian chair with cabriole legs, and start work at his heavy architects drawing board. Then, according to Illingworth:

> I drive up to London every Friday to Bouverie Street to show it to the editor and his executives who suggest what should be drawn. Sometimes I take up three or four samples. Only once did I have to follow their ideas.

Despite having to work again, and this time commute from the country, he still preferred to live and work in Sussex. Life in Sussex was now, according to Illingworth, "more violent than even in Wales. There is an atmosphere of lawlessness... you could be astounded by a new bug you've never seen before."

Neighbours in Robertsbride, East Sussex, Malcolm Muggeridge and Illingworth

In July 1975, Illingworth, to his immense surprise and delight, was granted the honorary degree of Doctor of Letters by the University of Kent at Canterbury, in recognition of his contribution to journalism. It was presented to him by the Chancellor Jo Grimond, the former leader of the Liberal Party. "They've started a cartoon archive there. I went up to Chancery Lane to be measured for my hat – I've a huge head. They've given me a degree not because I can read and write but because I can't!" In his address to the Chancellor, on this occasion the Public Orator, Professor W Hagenbach, described Illingworth as one of the most outstanding cartoonists of this century.

In June 1976, he retired again after suffering a minor stroke. He told his nephew that as a result of the stroke his "brain had gone" and he was no longer capable of producing a daily cartoon. His lifestyle was catching up with him. Illingworth had never held back on his liking for rich and fatty foods. He had once told Wally Fawkes at his dining table to "eat the fat, that's the best bit". Indulging himself in food and drink had obviously contributed to the thickening of his arteries. *Bristow* creator Frank Dickens noticed how 'red-faced' Illingworth always was. However, Illingworth was not entirely unhappy at having to retire as he now admitted to having become disillusioned with, or more likely had just tired of, the political scene. He believed that "biting, trenchant, bitter cartoons are no longer with us. Cartoons are an extension of politics and I think politics are finished now." It may be assumed that, being old school, he did not appreciate Gerald Scarfe and Ralph Steadman, whose work he would have regarded as too cruel and whose caricatures he would have considered too distorted to represent what he regarded as mainstream political caricature.

Illingworth was an incredibly modest man, believing he remained a better illustrator than a cartoonist and that his success as the latter had more to do with luck than judgement. In 1976, Illingworth stated that:

> I am not a good cartoonist. The cartoons I like best were those I liked drawing. For instance, the one about the cats and the goldfish. I think the drawing is very good. I should have been an illustrator...I would not select any cartoon as representative of my best work, only drawings, I was not a good cartoonist.

"I thought you said it was YOUR birthday, Harold"

News of the World
14 March 1976
Illingworth's rather respectful depiction of Conservative leader, Margaret Thatcher.

Although Illingworth never married, he loved the company of women, referring to himself as "an optimistic bachelor". He later put down never getting married to an early rejection, although somewhat tongue-in-cheek:

> I'm not a misogynist. I knew a delightful girl, born in Hawaii. She was delightful, she lived on a lovely farm in Wales, and I adored her. She was five, I was 15. I'd made up my mind. When she was 17 and I was 27 I asked her. And she said "No".

This in all probability disguises the fact that he neither wanted the commitment of a wife nor the loss of his own independence. The evidence appears to show that he *was* very much a misogynist. However, his relationship with Enid Ratcliff appears to have remained platonic throughout their years together. Her full-time role as housekeeper and confidante was all that he really needed from her. This seems to have been suggested in an interview she gave in the 1970s:

> We never quarrel, never at all. Not a bit like the state of matrimony. No sexual connections. I'm not the breeding type. They'd all come out with undershot jaws and two long arms.

Illingworth was also a romantic and refused to treat women in the same way as he did men in his cartoons. On the few occasions he felt he had to include female politicians such as Edith Summerskill, Barbara Castle and even Margaret Thatcher in his cartoons, he did so with great respect.

Illingworth's last published cartoon, drawn for a right-wing pressure group, appeared in the *Daily Telegraph* in 1977.

> I cannot caricature women. What I'd like to do is paint portraits in oils of beautiful young women. I like doing this very much.

Illingworth did have a network of female admirers, whose company he much enjoyed. They, in turn, became increasingly fond of him and treated him like a sort of genial uncle. These relationships, however, were certainly not just platonic. Illingworth once told Jim Hall, the son of his housekeeper, to get into the cupboard in his bedroom and watch him make love to one of his female admirers through the keyhole if the young lad wanted to learn all about the birds and the bees.

In 1976, Illingworth undertook a commission to draw some 25 illustrations for an American edition of *Ripples on the River* by Ewan Butler, which continued the characters of Rat, Mole and Toad from *Wind in the Willows* as defined by E H Shepard.

As Illingworth's heart condition worsened, Enid found that she could no longer look after him. There was therefore little choice but for him to be moved into a home in Hastings where, several months later, he died on 20 December 1979. On 31 December, a Church service was held for him in nearby Salehurst, immediately followed by his cremation at Hastings Crematorium. His ashes were scattered at the 'top field' at Silverdale. His old friend, Glyn Daniel, gave the address in which he described the calibre of the man

> There is a high place in heaven for the likes of him: not because of his skill and genius but because of his transparent goodness and integrity. Here was a man, admittedly with a genius for draughtsmanship, but to my way of thinking, an even greater genius for friendship. It has been said that friendship is a conspiracy for pleasure. If so, Leslie Illingworth was an arch-conspirator. He was the most friendly of men and never forgot any friends from whatever milieu they came. Here we are today – his friends from the Vale of Glamorgan, from Fleet Street, from Robertsbridge, to thank for his life of friendship and to do homage to him.

On 26 February 1980, a service of thanksgiving was held in St Bride's Church in Fleet Street, the spiritual home of journalism. In his obituary of Illingworth, Malcolm Muggeridge claimed that Illingworth's cartoons would, in the long run, wear better than David Low's because Low's cartoons related to an immediate situation which was soon forgotten, whereas, according to Muggeridge:

> Illingworth's went deeper, becoming at their best, satire in the grand style rather than mischievous quips; strategic rather than practical.

These were indeed kinds words by Muggeridge, who had a close and personal friendship with Illingworth. They had even been neighbours in Robertsbridge. Muggeridge, however, did seem to have a lifetime grudge against Low. He had written negatively about him whenever given the chance and his bigotry had once led him to describe Low as a 'crypto-Jew', which, of course, he was not. As a political cartoonist, Illingworth may have lacked the fierce partisan attack and reforming zeal of a David Low, a Vicky, or a Will Dyson, but his real strengths lay in his exquisite draughtsmanship and mastery of technique. He was the last of the great practitioners of penmanship and an undisputed master of scraperboard drawing. As a human being, he was loved by all. His generosity and his generosity of spirit knew no bounds. As we have seen he almost bankrupted himself because of it. Throughout his life, Illingworth appreciated his talents and the rewards that came from them. He enjoyed life to the full. To those who knew him, Illingworth made a habit of saying in his lilting Welsh accent: "How good it all is, Butty. Now. Not yesterday, tomorrow or next week but now." And for those that knew him, it always was.

Poy Returns to "The Daily Mail"

Poy, whose brilliant cartoons in the last war will be remembered by many thousands of readers, sends us the above. "The Daily Mail" hopes to publish more of his work from time to time.

5 September 1939
When war against Germany was declared on 3 September, the *Daily Mail* was still without a replacement for Percy Fearon (Poy), who had retired in February 1938. In desperation, the paper persuaded Poy to draw a weekly cartoon for them until they found a new political cartoonist.

HUMAN SACRIFICE
Harrowing picture of the Whitehall bureaucrats feeding their latest God

30 October 1939
This was Illingworth's first cartoon for the *Daily Mail*. During the First World War, Poy had pictured all Government control as needless interference in the lives of the public. Illingworth, obviously following the Editor's directive (there was a reference to 'this bloated octopus' of red tape in that day's *Daily Mail* leader), shows that at the start of this new war, things did not appear to have changed much. The Editor decided not to publish Illingworth's caption.

4 November 1939
President Roosevelt prevailed over the isolationists in the United States when he got the House of Congress to approve the 'Cash and Carry' Bill. This ended the arms embargo on Britain and France and allowed them to buy arms and munitions in the United States. One immediate effect was to make 800 planes available to Britain and France and with a positive spin, Illingworth believed, outweighed the advantages the Nazis had gained by their non-aggression pact with the Soviet Union.

NEUTRAL BALANCE OF THE WEEK

6 November 1939
In this cartoon, Illingworth again rather mendaciously criticises the Government's growing wartime interference in the economy as being a bad thing.

STATUE EXCAVATED IN WHITEHALL A.D. 1970

"Why so startled, Fuhrer? Don't you recognize one of your first members of the party."

10 November 1939
On 8 November, shortly after Hitler had made a speech at the *Burgerbraukeller* in Munich on the anniversary of the 1923 *Putsch*, a bomb exploded, wrecking the beer hall, killing eight people and injuring a further 60. The bomb had been hidden in a pillar immediately behind where Hitler had been speaking. After the explosion, the Ministry of Propaganda in Berlin insisted it knew nothing of the incident. Hitler saw his escape from injury and possible death as a sign of providence.

13 November 1939
Unlike the self-assured British Tommy in the famous First World War poster designed by Bert Thomas entitled *'Arf a Mo, Kaiser'*, who calmly lights his pipe before going 'over the top' to confront the German Hun, Hitler, having defeated Poland, seems quite unsure about what to do next.

THE NAZI WAR HORSE SORTS ITSELF OUT

17 November 1939
With Poland now occupied by Germany and the Soviet Union, Hitler and Stalin turned their attention towards the Balkan States. However, Romania and Greece had been given unilateral guarantees of military support by the British and French shortly after the dismemberment of Czechoslovakia. (In July 1940 this did not stop Romania from being forced to place herself under German protection.) According to Illingworth the composition of this cartoon was completely accidental:

> I was fiddling, doing little drawings of cats, goldfish and bowls, and suddenly there it was. I was not thinking of them at all. I was thinking of a little girl for whom I wanted to draw the cats and goldfish.

"WHAT, ME? NO, I NEVER TOUCH GOLDFISH"

BOOMERANG

20 November 1939
The Luftwaffe dropped magnetic mines in the Thames estuary, successfully sinking five merchant ships, including the minesweeper *Mastiff* on the day this cartoon was published. On 19 November, Winston Churchill, as First Lord of the Admiralty, recommended to the War Cabinet that Britain should retaliate by feeding "large numbers of floating mines into the Rhine River above Strasbourg".

WHY ARE THEY KEPT BEHIND BARS ?

28 November 1939
In 1935, Prime Minister Stanley Baldwin had appointed Ernest Brown as Minister of Labour. Brown now presided over a situation in which unemployment had increased as a result of cuts in government orders. This had had a particularly damaging effect on the building and associated trades as Britain turned its domestic economy into a wartime one.

4 December 1939
On 30 November, the Soviet Union invaded Finland after the Finns had refused to give in to Stalin's territorial demands. Under the secret protocol of the Nazi-Soviet Pact, the Germans had conceded the Baltic States (Estonia, Latvia, and Lithuania) and eastern Poland to the Soviet Union in return for the Soviets remaining neutral during the German invasion of Poland.

16 December 1939
This prophetic cartoon appeared a day before the German pocket battleship the *Admiral Graf Spee* left the harbour at Montevideo, only to be scuttled by its Captain Hans Langsdorff. A ruse by the British encouraged the Captain to think that he was outnumbered, with Royal Naval aircraft carriers and battleships on their way (in fact, not a single additional vessel could have arrived in time), and that his escape route was cut off. Captain Langsdorff committed suicide three days later. The crew of the *Graf Spee* was interned in Argentina and many stayed there even after 1945.

"AND I'VE PLENTY MORE POCKETS"

"YOU ARE UPHOLDING THE TRUEST TRADITIONS OF GERMAN WARRIORS"

22 December 1939
Illingworth draws a parallel between German atrocities already carried out in the war and the so-called infamous German atrocities of the First World War. During the German invasion of Poland, 'special action squads' of the SS and police were deployed behind the front lines, arresting and killing civilians considered, by virtue of their social status, to be capable of abetting resistance efforts against the Germans. Tens of thousands of former government officials, military officers in hiding, landowners, clergy, and members of the intelligentsia, Poles as well as Jews, were either murdered in mass executions by death squads or sent to prisons and concentration camps. "Whatever we find in the shape of an upper class in Poland will be liquidated," Hitler had ordered.

AN OUNCE OF HELP IS WORTH A TON OF PITY

29 December 1939
Stalin had expected to conquer the whole of Finland by the end of 1939, but despite numerical superiority, the Finnish Army not only held back the poorly led and poorly equipped Red Army but also inflicted heavy casualties upon it. Britain and France, observing the apparent weakness of the Red Army, debated sending troops to aid the Finns, and actually decided to do so a few days before a Soviet-Finnish peace treaty was concluded in March 1940.

"Have we hit something?"

8 January 1940
Leslie Hore-Belisha had been appointed Secretary of State for War on 25 May 1937. It had been a controversial appointment at the time, as most Conservatives were unhappy that such a high-profile appointment had not only gone to a National Liberal, but a Jew to boot! With the knowledge that a war was looming, Hore-Belisha set about modernising the British Army and improved living and working conditions for all ranks. The result was that recruitment rocketed with the Territorial Army doubling in size. As part of his modernisation plan, he also sacked three prominent members of the Imperial General Staff, replacing them with fresher minds. His attitude, however, alienated seasoned campaigners such as Field Marshals John Dill and John Gort. Hore-Belisha's changes also infuriated the establishment and this sentiment was passed down to the lower ranks. In the early months of the war, he banned a popular yet anti-Semitic song that had been widely sung by the armed forces, to the tune of "Onward, Christian Soldiers":

Onward Christian Soldiers
You have nothing to fear
Israel Hore-Belisha will lead
you from the rear
Clothed by Monty Burton
Fed on Lyons Pies
Die for Jewish freedom
As a Briton always dies

Under pressure from senior Conservatives, who believed that Hore-Belisha was more concerned in wanting Britain to wage war against Germany for the sole purpose of protecting European Jews, and the Imperial General Staff, Neville Chamberlain sacked Hore-Belisha on 4 January. Hore-Belisha is best remembered for introducing the Belisha beacon to British roads, named after him and as he appears in the cartoon as one.

AN APPLE FOR THE TEACHER

(The Government have decided that nearly half a million school children after their five months of war freedom must go back to school.)

10 February 1940
Almost a million schoolchildren were evacuated from British cities to places of safety in the countryside at the outbreak of war. When the expected bombing of cities did not take place, parents began to doubt whether they had made the right decision in sending away their children. By February 1940, many had already returned home.

"Only three cartridges – the rest are good will messages."

17 February 1940
Despite Finland's army mounting a spirited defence, the mobilization of further Soviet forces in February began to wear down Finnish resistance. The arrival of Marshal Timoshenko, with 27 new divisions, and armoured support enabled the Soviets to breach the Mannerheim Line on 11 February. Without Allied assistance, Finland was forced to seek an armistice on 6 March and a week later conceded all the territory and bases that the Soviets had originally demanded.

10 April 1940
The 'Phoney War' ended in the early morning of 9 April, not with a German attack on the Western Front but with the invasion of Denmark and Norway instead. This was ostensibly a pre-emptive manoeuvre against a planned Franco-British occupation of both these countries. The Norwegian Army was unable to stop the German advance despite British and French reinforcements, which were too little and too late. The campaign in southern Norway came to an end on 2 May with the evacuation of British and French forces and the surrender of the Norwegian Army. Then, and only then, did all eyes turn to the Franco-German border.

THE STARTER'S PISTOL

7 May 1940
On 5 April, Prime Minister Neville Chamberlain had felt sufficiently confident to declare to the House of Commons that Hitler had 'missed the bus'. However, he was made to eat his words after the military failure in Norway. There was now heightened dissatisfaction, and criticism of Chamberlain's conduct of the war. When Chamberlain entered the House of Commons on the day this cartoon appeared, many Labour MPs greeted him with shouts of: "Missed the bus! Missed the bus!"

THE BUS

TWO-GUN WINSTON

13 May 1940

On 8 May, the Labour Party demanded a debate on the unsuccessful Norwegian campaign, which turned into a vote of censure. At the end of the debate 30 Conservatives voted against Chamberlain and a further 60 abstained. The Labour Party also refused to join a Coalition Government under Chamberlain. As a result Chamberlain had little choice but to resign, which he did on 10 May. George VI appointed Winston Churchill as Prime Minister. Later that day the German Army began its Western Offensive and invaded the Netherlands, Belgium and Luxembourg. Two days later German forces entered France. Apart from Prime Minister, Churchill also appointed himself Minister for Defence at the head of a Defence Committee. On the day this cartoon was published, Churchill told the House of Commons:

> I would say to the House, as I said to those who have joined this Government: I have nothing to offer but blood, toil, tears and sweat.

15 May 1940
Within hours of the German *Blitzkrieg*, German panzer columns had driven through the wooded Ardennes, slicing through the Allied lines as they made their way relentlessly towards the Channel Ports. The Allies retreat was hindered by, Stuka dive-bombers, which strafed the refugee-crowded roads. The British Expeditionary Force and the remaining French forces were eventually pushed back into a shrinking perimeter around Dunkirk.

POINT-BLANK RANGE

12 June 1940
On 10 June, with France close to defeat and the British having successfully evacuated their forces from Dunkirk, Mussolini declared war on the Allies in the hope of sitting with Germany at the victor's table.

"WELCOME, BROTHER"

A TALE FROM 'ONE THOUSAND AND ONE NIGHTS'

RAF raids on Germany during the last three months have topped the 1,000 mark.

27 July 1940
Since the British army's retreat from Dunkirk in June, Bomber Command had become Britain's most potent offensive weapon. The RAF retaliated against the bombing of British cities by heavily bombing Berlin. Reichmarschall Hermann Goering, who was in overall command of the German Luftwaffe, had boasted that Berlin would not be subjected to a single bomb. "If an enemy bomber reaches Berlin, my name is not Hermann Goering: you can call me Meier!" (a German idiom to express that something is impossible.) By the end of the war, Berlin's air raid sirens were bitterly known to the city's residents as "Meier's trumpets" or "Meier's hunting horns."

FOSTER-MOTHER

23 August 1940
200 evacuee children arrived safely in New York on board the Cunarder Samaria. The ship had been delayed by fog and anxious members of the United States Committee for the Care of European Children had been keeping a nerve-racked vigil at the pier offices. Over the previous three days, 1,350 schoolchildren had also been evacuated to Canada under the British Government's scheme. The Children's Overseas Reception Board had been established in June 1940 and organised the evacuation of children to North America. When on 17 September, the SS City of Benares then sailing for Canada was torpedoed mid-Atlantic with the loss of 255 passengers, including 84 children, the great exodus ceased.

28 August 1940
On 23 August, German bombers attempting to bomb Rochester got lost and bombed London instead. In retaliation the British bombed Berlin. Infuriated by this, Hitler ordered the Luftwaffe to concentrate their bombing on London rather than British airfields. It proved to be a vital strategic error as it gave Fighter Command the time it needed to recover from both its losses and the exhaustion of its pilots.

"Tell me, Heinrich, what <u>does</u> a military objective look like??"

17 September 1940
The Germans realised that the RAF would have to be destroyed if any invasion of Britain was to succeed. Goering had promised Hitler that the Luftwaffe would destroy the RAF prior to any landings in Britain. During what became known as the Battle of Britain the Luftwaffe lost 1,389 planes compared to RAF losses of 792 planes. On the day this cartoon was published, Hitler postponed his planned invasion of Britain after failing to gain air supremacy over southern England.

Adolf: "I thought you had a winning system, Herman"

23 October 1940
For the first time since Marshal Pétain had surrendered on 22 June to the Germans, Winston Churchill, speaking in French, made a BBC short-wave broadcast to the French people in an attempt to inspire resistance against the Germans. "We are coming," he told them. The Germans tried unsuccessfully to jam the broadcast. Churchill's French won the praise of a Frenchman who told a *Daily Mail* reporter: "Your Prime Minister speaks excellently – with an accent, but not noticeably an English accent."

24 October 1940
Marshal Pétain appointed Pierre Laval as French Vice Premier and Foreign Minister. Laval's policy was active collaboration with Germany. He met Hitler in Montoire on 22 October and proposed an alliance between France and Germany. Two days later, he arranged the meeting between Pétain and Hitler in Montoire, where Vichy's collaborationist policy was ratified by a handshake between the two men. In fact the results of Montoire were a disappointment for both sides. Hitler failed in his attempt to get France to declare war on the British and the French failed to improve relations with her conqueror.

14 November 1940
On the nights of 11 and 12 November, British torpedo bombers from HMS Illustrious decimated the Italian Navy at Taranto Bay. Japanese planning staff studied the Taranto attack intensively when planning their successful attack on US naval forces at Pearl Harbor in 1941.

LIGHTS OUT IN THE WESTERN DESERT

38,114 prisoners captured.

30 December 1940
On 13 September, Italy's Tenth Army, stationed in Libya invaded the British protectorate of Egypt. Despite the British being outnumbered – 36,000 men compared to a total of 200,000 Italians, a counter-offensive on 9 December 1940 pushed the Italians back more than 500 miles to El Agheila, half way to Tripoli, as British troops moved westward along the North African coast.

"Tis a signpost your missing, Dev."

10 January 1941
The British Government offered to end the partition of Ireland in return for Eire's support in the war against Germany. Eire Prime Minister, Éamon de Valera, rejected the offer. De Valera followed a policy of strict neutrality for Ireland, refusing to let British forces use Irish naval bases, despite German air raids on the city of Dublin in 1941.

4 February 1941
After winning the election in November 1940, President Roosevelt introduced a 'Lend-Lease' Act into Congress in January 1941, empowering him to sell or lend military equipment vital to Britain's war effort. In a 'fireside chat' broadcast to the American people, Roosevelt explained his reasoning: "Your neighbour's house is on fire. He comes to you and asks if he can have your hose. You say 'I will not give you my hose but I will lend it to you. You can borrow it to put out your fire. And when the fire is out, you will return it to me.'"

STATUTE OF LIBERTY

12 February 1941
On 21 January, King Boris III endorsed the newly enacted 'Law for the Protection of the Nation', which mimicked Nazi Germany's Nuremburg Laws in stripping Bulgaria's Jews of their property, livelihood, education and dignity. Then on 1 March, King Boris III formally brought Bulgaria into an alliance with Nazi Germany and the other Axis powers.

15 April 1941
To bolster the faltering Italians in North Africa, Hitler sent General Erwin Rommel, The Desert Fox, with two armoured divisions of the Afrika Korps. On 14 February, Rommel and his forces arrived in Tripoli. Although originally intended to be only a small blocking force, by 15 April Rommel had pushed the British eastward all the way back to the Egyptian border.

1 May 1941
Information on Hitler's intention to invade the Soviet Union came to Stalin from various sources. Churchill sent a personal message to Stalin in April explaining how German troop movements suggested that they were about to launch an attack. However, Stalin was still suspicious of the British and thought that Churchill was trying to trick him into declaring war on Germany. Stalin even decided to ignore one of his top spies, Richard Sorge, after he had informed him of the exact date of the German invasion. Stalin also ignored reports directly from the border regions of large German troop concentrations, and ordered his soldiers not to open fire on German aircraft that were routinely violating Soviet airspace to stage brazen reconnaissance missions.

10 May 1941
Despite the threat of Nazi Germany, an overwhelming majority of Americans wanted to stay out of the war in Europe if they could. In contrast, American Secretary of War Henry Stimson delivered a speech to Congress on 7 May calling on the full use of the United States Navy against the Axis:

> The world is facing so great a crisis that all of our efforts must be turned toward the defence of our nation's safety. Our own self-defence requires that limits should be put to lawless aggression on the ocean. The President has said that we must not allow the steps that we have already taken to become ineffective.

GULLIVER AWAKES

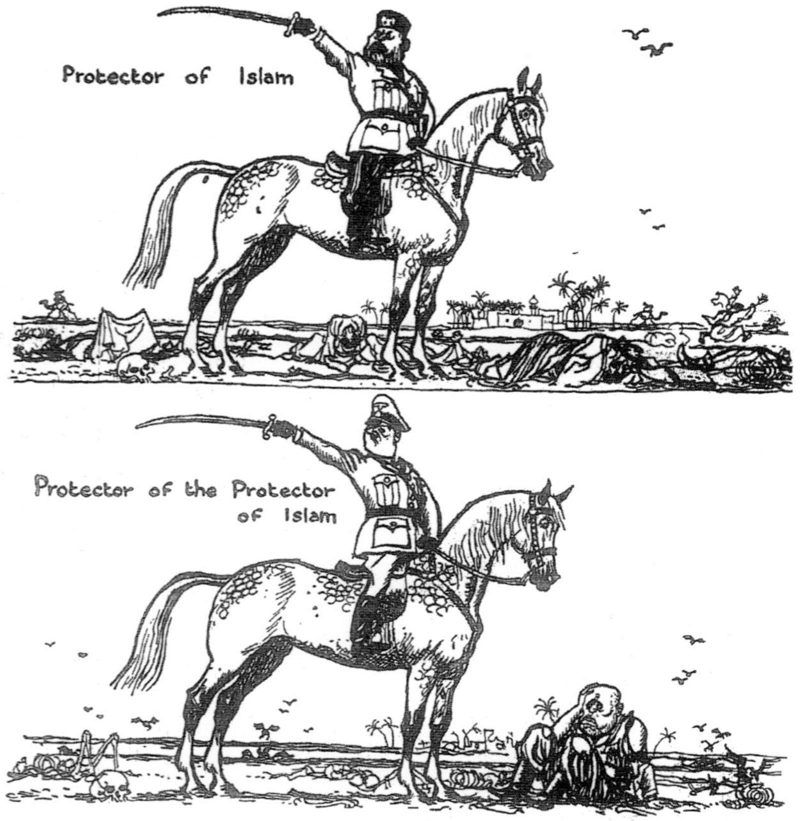

19 May 1941
By May, the British had overrun Benito Mussolini's East African Empire of Somaliland, Eritrea and Abyssinia, where the deposed ruler Haile Selassie was restored to power. Hitler also scolded his Axis partner, Mussolini, for his troops' retreat in the face of British advances in Libya, North Africa. As Britain threatened to push the Italians out of Libya altogether and break through to Tunisia, Mussolini swallowed his pride and asked Hitler for assistance. It was only with the arrival of German forces under Rommel that the British advance was halted.

23 June 1941
On 22 June, Hitler broke the Nazi-Soviet Pact and invaded the Soviet Union. Stalin had avoided any obvious defensive preparations in case it provoked the Germans. As a result, the Soviet Army was unprepared for the onslaught. Even hours after the initial German attack, Stalin hesitated, wanting to ensure that it had been sanctioned by Hitler, rather than the unauthorised action of a rogue general.

19 July 1941
Spanish Dictator General Franco felt immensely confident about the outcome of the war. In his most openly pro-Axis speech of the war, and on the fifth anniversary of the Nationalist rising, Franco freely admitted Spain's involvement in the war against the Soviet Union by boasting, "The blood of our youth is to mingle with that of our comrades of the Axis". Franco grandly announced:

> I do not harbour any doubts whatsoever about the result of the war. The die is cast, and the first battle was won here in Spain. The war is lost for the Allies. France and every people in the continent of Europe realise it. There is no mortal force that can change the destiny to come.

Referee ('The Allies Have Lost Already') Franco

28 July 1941
On 25 July, the United States denounced Japan's invasion of French Indochina. President Roosevelt attempted to deter the Japanese from further aggression by not only freezing Japanese assets in the United States and forbidding Japanese ships passage through the Panama Canal, but by also putting General Douglas MacArthur in charge of the newly established US Army in the Far East.

KEEPING STEP

ONE DOWN AND TWO TO GO

17 September 1941
Britain and the Soviet Union, fearing that the Shah of Iran was about to align his oil-rich country with Germany, invaded Iran and deposed the Shah. They had already been alarmed at his earlier Declaration of Neutrality as well as his refusal to allow Iranian territory to be used as a transport corridor to ship arms to Russia. The Shah's son, Mohammad Reza Pahlavi, officially replaced his father on the throne on 16 September.

THE LEARNER

19 November 1941
The German Army was only 19 miles from Moscow when the mud and the Russian winter weather, the worst in 20 years, stopped it in its tracks. Having expected a rapid Soviet collapse, German planners had failed to equip their troops for winter warfare. The German tanks could not handle the subzero temperatures. Fires had to be set under the engines to help start them. The few heaters they had were used on the engines even though the mechanics' hands froze to their tools. The Germans would never reach Moscow.

4 December 1941
Japan assured the United States that its build-up of troops in Indochina was purely a defensive measure.

LOITERING WITH INTENT

DEATH TAKES A HOLIDAY

9 December 1941
On 7 December, the Japanese launched a surprise attack on the United States naval base at Pearl Harbor. The attack led to President Roosevelt declaring war on the Japanese, stating that 7 December 1941 was a date that would live in "infamy". On 11 December, Hitler declared war on the United States, despite being under no obligation to do so under the mutual defence terms of the Tripartite Pact. Hitler awarded Imperial Japanese ambassador to Nazi Germany Hiroshi Oshima the Grand Cross of the Order of the German Eagle in Gold after the attack on Pearl Harbor.

11 December 1941
On 10 December, 27 bombers of the Japanese Air Force attacked the British battleship HMS Prince of Wales and the battle cruiser HMS Repulse. Without air cover the two ships had little chance of surviving. Both ships were sunk with the total loss of 840 British sailors. With Germany having declared war on the United States and the Japanese having declared war on the British, the Western Democracies now stood shoulder to shoulder determined to defeat the Axis powers.

13 December 1941
With America and the Soviet Union as Allies, Britain's military position looked far less precarious than it had a year earlier when it fought the Axis powers alone. On 6 December, the Red Army counterattacked along the three fronts that intersected Moscow. In Libya, British and Australian troops were on the verge of retaking Benghazi, although it was to change hands five times as the North African campaign ebbed and flowed along the Mediterranean coast.

OVER ON THE BRIGHT SIDE

2 January 1942
While the war appeared to be going against Germany in both North Africa and in Russia, the Japanese advance in the Far East continued unabated. On 18 December 1941 they took Penang, a week later they captured Hong Kong.

28 January 1942
After two and a half years of war and without a major victory against the Germans, there were politicians from all three major political parties as well as a hostile press criticising Churchill for Britain's lack of military success. On 27 January, with mounting opposition, Churchill called for a vote of confidence in the House of Commons. He won the vote overwhelmingly by 484 to 1 and noted after the vote that "the naggers in the Press spun around with the alacrity of squirrels".

FUN WHILE IT LASTS

18 February 1942
Illingworth's cartoon attempts to make light out of one of Britain's worst military defeats in its history: the loss of Singapore to the Japanese army on 15 February. A strategically vital military base that protected Britain's possessions in the Far East, it had supposedly been an impregnable fortress.

16 February 1942
As losses to merchant shipping in the Atlantic escalated, the Allies faced the real possibility that Britain could be forced into capitulation. Many cartoonists, as Illingworth has done here, focussed their criticism on those deemed to be wasting valuable resources that had been brought to this country at great cost, especially in the lives of merchant seaman. A cartoon by Philip Zec on the same issue almost got the *Daily Mirror* closed down by the British Government.

PAYING FOR IT

11 March 1942
The Japanese army, having captured Hong Kong from the British, carried out atrocities to both Allied prisoners of war and the indigenous civil population. Many British soldiers were tied to trees and then bayoneted to death. The term 'bushido', literally translated as 'the way of the warrior', described the samurai code of ethics in the 17th century. To Japanese troops who had been taught that surrender was dishonourable, Allied prisoners appeared as nothing less than cowards.

BASHIDO – THE WAY OF A WARRIOR

OUT OF DANGER?

29 May 1942
Reinhard Heydrich was second only to Heinrich Himmler in the SS. As Deputy Reich Protector of Bohemia and Moravia he conducted a brutal crackdown of the Czech resistance movement. Heydrich also chaired the 1942 Wannsee Conference, which discussed plans for the deportation and extermination of all Jews in German-occupied territory. On 27 May, Heydrich was attacked by assassins in Prague and died over a week later from complications arising from his injuries.

DON'T WORRY HIM, BOYS – HE PROMISED YOU SHALL GO

29 July 1942
Despite Stalin's demands for a Second Front, and unlike in this cartoon, Churchill believed that the Allies were unprepared for an invasion of northern France in 1942. To do so, according to Churchill, would have ended in disaster. He argued: "War was war but not folly, and it would be folly to invite a disaster which would help nobody." Instead, he thought it better to exploit recent successes in North Africa. In August, Churchill flew to Moscow to tell Stalin that there would be no Second Front in Western Europe that year. Stalin condemned the decision to abandon the Second Front stating, "A man who was not prepared to take risks could not win a war."

3 August 1942

The German summer offensive in the East began in June. By the end of July, German forces had reached the Don River bend west of Stalingrad.

8 August 1942

With Japanese troops getting ever closer to India's borders, Mahatma Gandhi called for a massive civil disobedience campaign throughout India in order to bring about the immediate end of British rule. The Indian Congress had also, on the same day, passed by a 20–1 majority a 'Quit India' resolution. The British authorities reacted by arresting Gandhi and many other Congress leaders and officials.

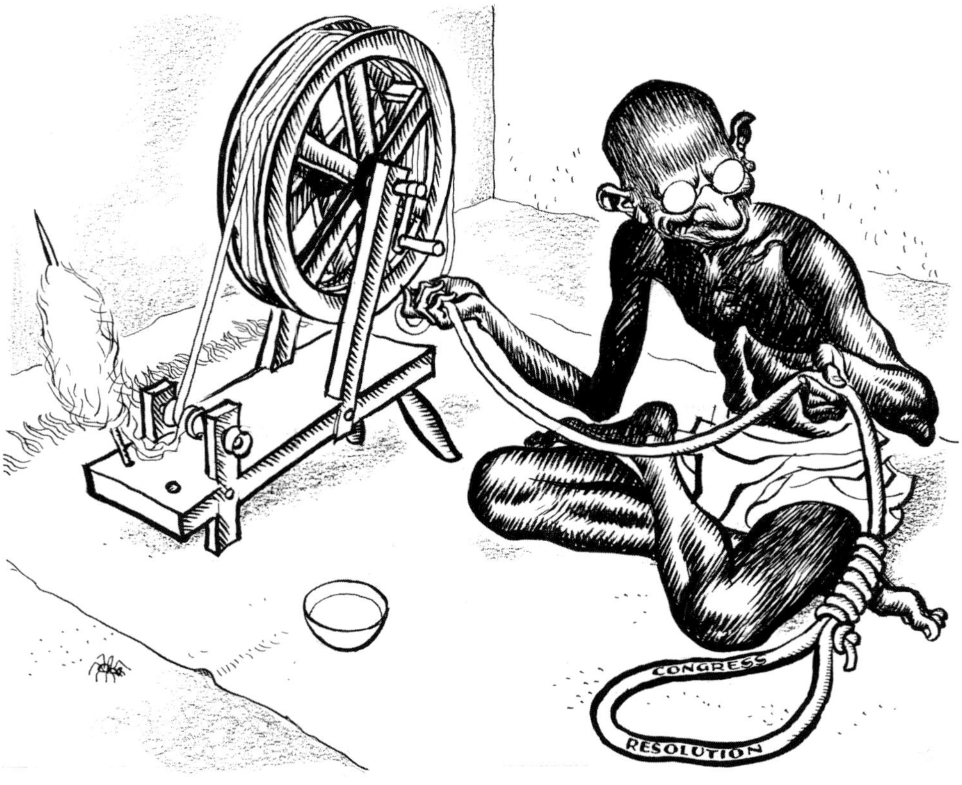

A PRESENT FOR MOTHER INDIA

SECOND THOUGHTS

10 October 1942
On 21 August, the Germans reached Stalingrad, the city named after Stalin as a result of his defence of the city during the Russian Civil War. Stalin insisted that the city should be held at all costs. One historian has claimed that he saw Stalingrad "as the symbol of his own authority". Stalin also knew that if Stalingrad were taken, the way would be open for Moscow to be attacked from the east. If Moscow was cut off in this way, the defeat of the Soviet Union was virtually inevitable. The battle for Stalingrad was marked by brutality and disregard for military and civilian casualties on both sides. As the German army advanced the Soviets fought for every building. The deeper the Germans got into the city, the more difficult the street fighting became and their casualties increased dramatically. By October, the Germans had lost 40,000 men since entering the city. On 4 October, due to the high casualty rate, General Paulus made a desperate plea to Hitler for reinforcements.

20 October 1942
Illingworth foresees the American landing in Vichy-held French North Africa in November 1942. The Americans expected little or no resistance from Vichy French forces and were surprised by the strong resistance put up by them when they landed in Oran and Morocco. In Algiers, due to a *coup d'état* by the French resistance, the landings met no practical opposition and the city was captured on the first day along with the entire Vichy African command. However, unlike in the cartoon, the Americans did not, in fact, land in Liberia, despite signing a defence pact with that country.

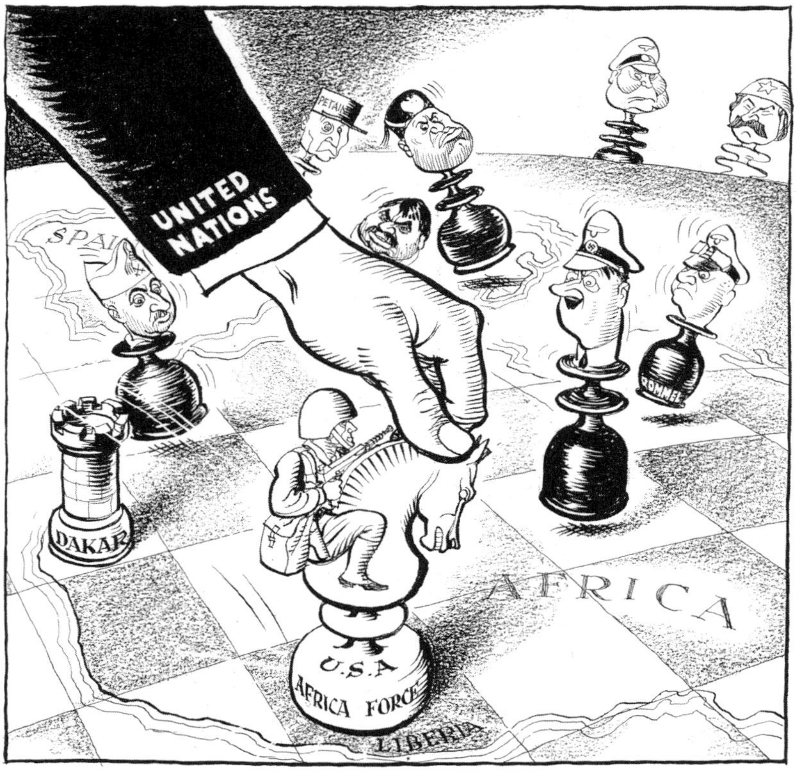

CHECK!

4 November 1942
The Battle of El Alamein marked the turning point in Britain's fortunes in the Second World War. There were three separate battles between July and November 1942, all of which were fought to halt the advance of Rommel's army towards the Suez Canal. This final battle at El Alamein, fought in November, saw the continuous bombardment of the German line that Rommel was instructed to hold at all costs by Hitler himself. The Allies shattered the German defences, which led to Rommel leading a westward retreat in order to salvage what was left of the Afrika Korps. Churchill was convinced that the Battle of El Alamein marked the turning point in the war and ordered the ringing of church bells all over Britain. As he said later: "Before Alamein we never had a victory, after Alamein we never had a defeat."

SNAKE, SWAN – OR TIMEBOMB?

23 November 1942
The Beveridge Report was presented to Parliament by its author, Sir William Beveridge. It provided a summary of principles necessary to banish poverty and 'want' from Britain. The paper proposed a system of social security that would be operated by the state, to be implemented once the war was over. Inside the Cabinet there was much debate, instigated by Brendan Bracken on 16 November, over whether to publish the Report as a White Paper at that time. The Chancellor of the Exchequer, Sir Kingsley Wood, believed the Report to be "ambitious and involving an impracticable financial commitment" and therefore publication should be postponed.

27 November 1942
The temperatures, so far relatively mild by Russian standards, dropped as low as 20 to 50 degrees Celsius below zero. German troops, who still had no winter clothing, and German vehicles that were not designed for such severe weather, could not cope and froze. More than 130,000 cases of frostbite were reported among German soldiers. Frozen grease had to be removed from every loaded shell and vehicles had to be heated for hours before use. The Axis offensive on Moscow stopped. As General Guderian wrote in his journal, 'The offensive on Moscow failed. We underestimated the enemy's strength, as well as his size and climate.'

12 December 1942
The *Daily Mail* ran a campaign against the Ministry of Home Security's regulations that the paper felt made blackout railway travel 'difficult and dangerous'. The paper called for better lighting in trains and on station platforms during the blackout hours, especially as they believed the black-out offered no security against bombing and was responsible for many casualties amongst railway passengers.

Is his journey really necessary?

14 December 1942
In the course of 1942 various accounts of Nazi atrocities against the Jews circulated. A week after this cartoon appeared, Foreign Secretary Anthony Eden told a shocked House of Commons that according to Polish sources, mass executions of Jews were taking place in occupied Europe, that Jewish ghettoes were being 'systematically emptied' and that the able-bodied were being sent to labour camps. After his announcement the House rose and held a one-minute silence in sympathy for the victims.

"DRANG NACH OSTEN"

2 February 1943
Drang nach Osten is German for 'Drive to the East', the Nazi policy to colonise the Slavic lands east of Germany. The phrase occurred in Hitler's tirades against Czechoslovakia during the late 1930s. On 30 January, Hitler promoted von Paulus to Field Marshal and sent him a message reminding him that no German Field Marshal had ever been taken alive. Hitler was clearly suggesting to Paulus to commit suicide but he declined and the following day surrendered to the Red Army. According to recent estimates 60,000 Germans died in Stalingrad and 110,000 went into Soviet captivity. The German prisoners were forced marched to Siberia. About 45,000 died during the march to the prisoner of war camps and only about 7,000 survived the war.

MORE AMMO! QUICK, MORE AMMO!

5 February 1943
German forces and their allies had suffered very heavy casualties at Stalingrad including many Italian, Hungarian and Romanian troops. These were losses that Germany and her allies would not be able to recover from.

3 March 1943

In February, Gandhi, who was still imprisoned, started a 21-day fast. The popular response to the news of Gandhi's fast led to demonstrations and strikes throughout India. Prisoners went on sympathetic hunger strikes. By the twelfth day of the fast, Gandhi was in a grave condition and nearly died. However, Churchill like Illingworth was unsympathetic over Gandhi's hunger strike 'antics'. "The old rascal," according to Churchill, "has not the slightest intention of dying." Churchill was later informed that Gandhi had cheated by taking glucose in his water and was slipped the occasional orange juice when he looked groggy. On 1 March, Gandhi ended his fast.

16 April 1943

As Italian forces surrendered in North Africa and the Allies prepared to invade the Italian island of Sicily, Mussolini's regime came under increasing pressure. Mussolini's once ubiquitous propaganda machine had also lost its grip on the Italian people, with a large number of them turning to Vatican Radio or Radio London for more accurate news coverage. Mussolini is pictured here with his daughter Edda and son-in-law and Italian Foreign Minister Count Gian Galeazzo Ciano.

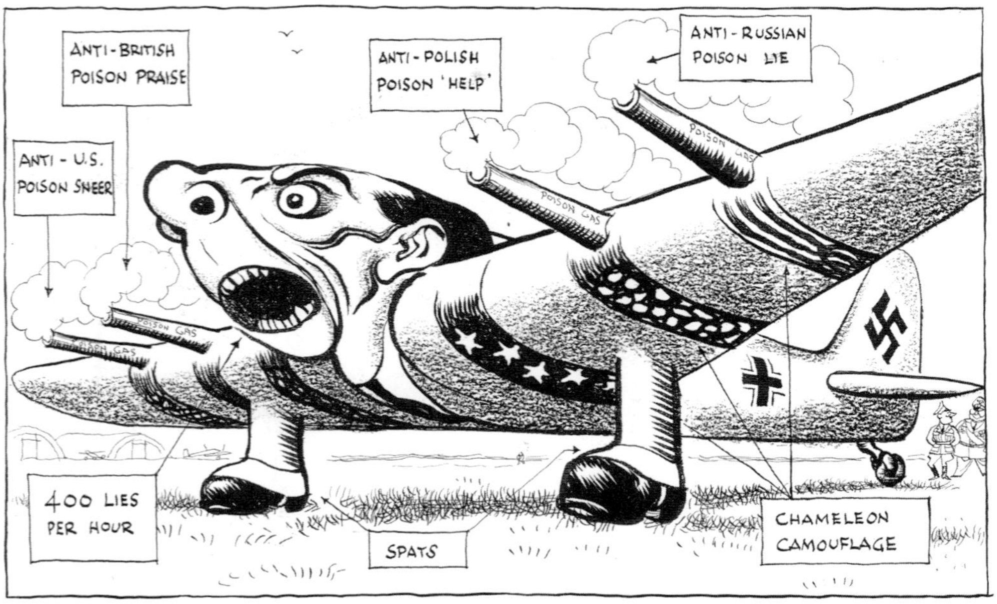

THE LIE-PHOON

30 April 1943
The Hawker Typhoon came into its own as a ground attack aircraft and was used to launch attacks on the German transport system in occupied France, becoming especially adept at destroying railway trains. By 1943, Nazi Propaganda Minister Dr Joseph Goebbels was firmly associated with conjuring lies and deceit in his propaganda broadcasts. He once said that "A lie repeated a thousand times becomes a truth."
As with Illingworth's version of the 'Lie-Phoon', Goebbels wore spats to hide the fact that he had one leg shorter than the other.

17 May 1943
Illingworth reworks an earlier cartoon (see page 42) to show how the tables had been turned on the Nazis. On 16 May, the RAF launched what became known as the *Dambusters Raid* in the industrial heartland of Germany. The raid successfully damaged three dams serving the Ruhr valley.

25 June 1943
Sir Arthur 'Bomber' Harris laid claim to being one of the principal architects of the Allied victory over Germany. Harris believed implicitly that Germany's morale could be broken and its capacity for waging war wrecked by the systematic destruction of its industrial base, production facilities and city centres by huge Allied bombing raids.

AN EXPIREMENT WELL WORTH TRYING

17 July 1943
On 16 July, Churchill and Roosevelt made a radio broadcast to the Italian people, calling on them not to die for Hitler but to "live for civilisation". On the same day, the Italian Fascist leaders opposed to Mussolini began to agitate for his removal.

– AND THEY ALWAYS GET THEIR MAN

13 August 1943
A meeting of the Fascist Grand Council was held on 24 July, at which Mussolini's former Fascist colleagues turned against him. The following day King Victor Emmanuel III told Mussolini he was dismissed from office. His successor, Pietro Badoglio, declared martial law and placed Mussolini under arrest. Churchill flew to meet Roosevelt and Canadian Prime Minister Mackenzie King in Quebec City, where they would discuss the bombing offensive against Germany and the continued build-up of American forces in Britain prior to an invasion of France.

THE PROMISED LAND

23 August 1943
The RAF carried out its first 'obliteration' raid on Berlin. This was the start of Air Marshall Sir Arthur Harris' six-month bombing campaign to "wreck Berlin from end to end".

6 September 1943
On 3 September, British and Canadian troops of the Eighth Army under General Bernard Montgomery executed *Operation Baytown*, crossing the Strait of Messina into Calabria. Opposition to the landings was light; with Italian units surrendering almost immediately. On 8 September, Italy surrendered to the Allies. However, the German forces in Italy were prepared for such an eventuality, quickly disarming the Italians and taking control of the defence of the Italian peninsula. Hitler gave Field Marshal Albert Kesselring responsibility for defending southern Italy.

YOU'D BETTER NOT ROLL THOSE BLUE, BLUE EYES AT ANYONE ELSE THAN ME...?

21 September 1943
Churchill returned from a six-week trip to the United States and Canada. It had been his longest period away yet since becoming Prime Minister. Chancellor of the Exchequer and a member of the War Cabinet, Sir Kingsley Wood, portrayed rather 'spookily' here with a halo above his head, was working on his 'pay as you earn' tax system when he died suddenly on the day this cartoon was published.

Look out chaps... the Head!

Falling Idol

25 October 1943
The Red Army launched an offensive across the Dnieper River in a bid to retake Kiev from the Germans. The 'Battle of the Lower Dnieper' was one of the largest battles of the war, involving almost four million troops on both sides and stretching over a front a mile long. At the end of the offensive, Soviet forces gained control of the Dneiper, cutting the Crimea off from the rest of the German forces.

20 December 1943
The first German war criminals of the Second World War were given a four-day trial at the Kharkov theatre in Ukraine, before a capacity audience of 6,000. In the dock were three German soldiers, Corporal Reinhard Retzlav, 36, of the secret field police; Hans Ritz, 24, of the Kharkov Gestapo; and Captain Wilhelm Langheld, 52, of the army's secret service. The fourth man was a Russian spy, Mikhail Bulanov, who had assisted the Gestapo in Kharkov while working as a driver for the Germans. The four men were found guilty of helping to gas "peaceful Soviet citizens" in mobile gas chambers on the backs of lorries, and the three Germans were also accused of torturing Russians with red-hot pokers. All four were hanged publicly in Kharkov's central square on 19 December.

COMING EVENTS

THE LAST ACT

22 December 1943
Stalin, Roosevelt and Churchill met in Tehran to discuss the opening of a second front in Western Europe. Roosevelt gave Stalin a pledge that he had been waiting for since June 1941: that the Anglo-Americans would open a second front in France in the spring of 1944. Operation Overlord was scheduled to begin in May 1944, in conjunction with the Soviet attack on Germany's eastern border.

THE RIGHT TONIC

28 December 1943
After his exhausting trip to the Middle East, Churchill contracted pneumonia. He became rather perturbed at his condition for it was the first time he had been seriously ill since he had had his appendix removed in 1922. His doctor's reassured him that a new 'M & B' drug now made pneumonia a much more manageable illness. On 26 December, Germany's 26,000-ton battleship Scharnhorst was sunk by British cruisers protecting a Russian convoy on the northern route to Murmansk. 1,932 crewmembers were lost whilst only 36 crew members survived.

3 January 1944
On 4 January, the Red Army, led by General Vatutin, crossed the Polish frontier from Ukraine. The severely depleted German forces could do little to halt the Soviet advance. Stalin was determined not to give back anything that had been gained due to his agreement with the Nazis. The ultimate goal of Stalin was to move the Polish eastern border to the Curzon line and the western border to the Oder-Neisse line.

CONTINUOUS PERFORMANCE

31 January 1944
As Soviet Forces advanced westwards, Hitler gave a rare radio broadcast, laying most of the emphasis in his speech on the "Communist danger" threatening Europe:

> Germany in this war is struggling not only for herself but for all Europe. One thing is certain. There will only be one victor in this war and that will be either Germany or Soviet Russia. A German victory will mean the maintenance of Europe; a Russian victory will mean Europe's annihilation. This must be obvious to anyone unless he is stark mad. If Germany does not win, the fate of Europe will be sealed in a matter of months.

WHO'S AFRAID?

OH, COME OFF IT?

2 February 1944
Under threat of an oil embargo by the Roosevelt administration, the Spanish government agreed to restrict the shipment of raw materials to Germany as well as to limit the activities of Axis agents in Spain.

HIS EASTER BONNET

8 April 1944
200,000 coalminers went on strike in the coal-mining regions of South Wales and Yorkshire. The strikes were blamed on the Trotskyites by the President of the Miners' Union, William Lawther. The *Daily Mail* published a sensational exposé by one of its reporters, who claimed to have formed a team of special investigators all over the country tracking down Trotskyites. Minister of Labour, Ernest Bevin, took up the theme, accusing the followers of Leon Trotsky who, he claimed, not only had plenty of members and money, but "more influence among certain sections of the workers than His Majesty's Government and the trade union leaders combined". As a consequence, a new regulation, opposed by the Unions, was passed, giving the Government power to imprison or fine those responsible for 'inciting strikes and lockouts which interfere with essential services.'

25 May 1944
On 24 May, Churchill made a foreign policy speech in the House of Commons in which, to the surprise and dismay of many, he praised the Fascist leaderships of Spain's General Franco and Italy's Marshal Badoglio in the hope of pacifying them. Meanwhile preparations for the forthcoming Allied landings in Normandy continued. During the speech, Churchill also explained why he had not officially recognised the French Committee of National Liberation under the leadership of General Charles De Gaulle. He felt that it would be wrong to impose the French Committee upon all of France without more knowledge of how the occupied French felt about the Committee.

29 May 1944
The Allies had landed troops on the west coast of Italy at Anzio in January with the intention of breaking the deadlock in the Italian campaign. However, Allied troops suffered heavy casualties from Field Marshall Kesselring's troops and it was only after reinforcements arrived that they succeeded in breaking out from the beachhead and linking up with the US 5th Army on 25 May. The 5th Army under Lieutenant-General Mark Clark pressed on to take Rome on 4 June, ignoring orders from General Alexander to thrust into the German line of retreat. The capture of Rome was seen as significant but it meant the Germans were able to escape.

ROMAN HOLIDAY

7 June 1944
On 6 June, D Day, the Allied invasion of Northern France successfully took place, beginning the liberation of mainland Europe from Nazi occupation.

YES, ADOLF; THIS IS IT!

20 June 1944
On 13 June, a week after the D-Day landings, Hitler unleashed his "vengeance weapon" on London. The V.1's, which commonly became known as the 'doodlebug', were launched from ramps located along the Belgium coast and the Pas de Calais in France. At the height of the V.1 blitz in late June, as many as 100 were reaching London every day. The odd "Putt Putt" sound of an approaching V.1 meant that Londoners learned almost to ignore their presence until the sudden absence of that sound; knowing that as long as they could hear that distinctive sound they were safe. Once its engine cut out, they had about 15 seconds to find safety before the explosion.

...AFTER THE LIGHT IS SEEN TO GO OUT, THE MACHINE DIVES STEEPLY AND EXPLODES ON STRIKING THE GROUND.

22 July 1944
After the attempt to assassinate Hitler on 20 July failed, Himmler's Gestapo rounded up nearly everyone who had had the remotest connection with the plot. Under Himmler's new Sippenhaft blood guilt laws, all the relatives of the principal plotters were also arrested. Eventually some 5,000 people were arrested and about 200 were executed. Not all of them were connected with the 20 July plot, since the Gestapo used the occasion to settle scores with many other people suspected of opposition sympathies. Very few of the plotters tried to escape or to deny their guilt when arrested. Those who survived interrogation were given perfunctory trials before the People's Court and its notorious judge Roland Freisler. Hitler ordered that those found guilty were to be "hung like cattle".

THE END IN SIGHT

23 August 1944
After more than four years of Nazi occupation, Paris was liberated by the French 2nd Armoured Division and the U.S. 4th Infantry Division. German resistance was light, and General Dietrich von Choltitz, commander of the German garrison, defied an order by Hitler to blow up Paris' landmarks and burn the city to the ground before its liberation. On 26 August, Free French General Charles de Gaulle led a joyous liberation march down the Champs d'Elysées.

Hitler: 3 New Stories

'Operation' Theory

NEW stories of what has happened to Hitler reached London last night. All were unconfirmed—and Berlin is still attempting to persuade the world that there is no mystery in the Führer's prolonged "absence."

Here are the stories:

1 The Führer is at Berchtesgaden, where he has been operated upon for a throat tumour. His condition is said to be such that he needs "constant attention."

This report came from a high German official in Switzerland.

2 The real Hitler is now under close watch by Himmler, who plotted the Führer's death in the July 20 bomb conspiracy but only succeeded in killing his double.

This account comes from a German "Social Democrat," now safe in a neutral country.

3 Hitler is alive and well and Berlin produces proof of it in the shape of photographs showing him decorating soldiers.

But Swiss reports say that great consternation has been caused in Germany because it is known that many of the men were killed some time ago.

Daily Mail Article
14 November 1944

NO TIME FOR DREAMS

15 November 1944
After the German defeat at Stalingrad, Hitler became something of a recluse and began to avoid public appearances and making radio broadcasts. On 14 November, a proclamation was issued to the German people in Hitler's name by Heinrich Himmler in a radio broadcast that would normally have been performed by Hitler himself. The *Daily Mail* referred to the growing mystery of Hitler's disappearance as 'Hypnotic voice has lost grip on people'.

ALWAYS WORTH TRYING

7 November 1944
General Franco pleaded for a place at the eventual peace conference for 'neutral countries' (meaning Spain) and spoke of "their serene and disinterested understanding of what is just". Spanish officials also rather disingenuously argued that Spain had never been anything other than a neutral bystander during the war and that its Catholic nature had made it incompatible with the totalitarianism of the Axis.

HIS LAST ALLY

20 November 1944
Allied troops were forced to fight the retreating Germans in freezing sleet, in rain and in snow as they made their way slowly eastwards.

7 December 1944
Although Greece was liberated from German occupation, a civil war broke out between Greek Communists (ELAS), and nationalist forces (EDES). On 3 December, during a demonstration in Athens, involving more than 100,000 people, fighting broke out that led to the deaths of 28 people and 148 being injured. This signalled the beginning of the 'Dekemvriana' (the December events), a 37-day period of full-scale fighting in Athens between ELAS and EDES. The British tried to stay neutral, but when the battle escalated they intervened to try to stop the rival combatants from causing further bloodshed.

18 December 1944
Sources in Washington stated that Churchill, Stalin and Roosevelt would meet early in 1945 after the President's fourth term inauguration. The venue had yet to be decided with the Foreign Secretary, Anthony Eden, suggesting it be held in Britain as "the Prime Minister is the oldest of these men". The 'Big Three' conference was eventually held in February in the Livadia Palace near Yalta in the Crimea. Each leader had an agenda for the Yalta Conference: Roosevelt asked for Soviet support in the war against Japan; Churchill pressed for free elections and democratic governments in Eastern Europe (specifically Poland); and Stalin demanded a Soviet sphere of political influence in Eastern Europe, as essential to the USSR's national security.

REMOTE CONTROL

TESTING TIME

22 December 1944
On 16 December, under cover of heavy fog, Field Marshall von Rundstedt launched a powerful counteroffensive in the wooded Ardennes region of southern Belgium initially catching American troops off guard. The German advance led to a significant 'bulge' in the Allied line. The German Army managed to push American forces back nearly to the Meuse River and surround the town of Bastogne in Belgium. When ordered to surrender Bastogne, Brigadier General Anthony C McAuliffe famously replied: "Nuts!"

HAUNTED HEADQUARTERS

10 January 1945
As the Ardennes crisis deepened, General Montgomery assumed temporary command of the American First and Ninth Armies, launching a counter-offensive against the Germans on 3 January. On the same day as Hitler's withdrawal order on 7 January, Montgomery held a press conference in which he said he had "headed off , seen off and written off" the Germans.

14 February 1945
At the Yalta Conference, Roosevelt, Churchill, and Stalin confirmed the policy adopted at the Casablanca Conference of demanding Germany's unconditional surrender.

NO REPRIEVE

16 February 1945
This scraperboard drawing accompanied an article in the *Daily Mail* entitled 'White girl, yellow prison'. This was, according to the paper, the first authentic account ever to emerge of a 3-year term in a Japanese prison-camp for civilians by the first Englishwomen released when the American forces of liberation reached Santo Tomas. In the article it stated that:

> We made up the lack of protein in the Jap diet with cats, dogs, snails and grubs. Maybe it was the heartbreaking sound of children crying for food that was not there that sent their mothers scavenging for discarded vegetable peel among the kitchen garbage. Anyway whatever the cause, they did it.

MOTHERS SCAVENGED AMONG THE GARBAGE.

TO LAST 1,000 YEARS?

2 April 1945
At the beginning of April, Hitler moved into the Führerbunker, located 50 feet below the Chancellery buildings in Berlin. Hitler held daily briefings with his generals amid reports of the unstoppable Soviet advance into Berlin. He issued frantic orders to defend Berlin with armies that were already wiped out or were making a hasty retreat westward to surrender to the Americans. This is a rather prophetic cartoon considering that on 30 April he did in fact commit suicide by shooting himself in the mouth with a pistol.

13 April 1945
According to the *Daily Mail*, American airborne troops who captured the German town of Essen were met by "Welcome" signs and German civilians, who threw their arms around the troops and offered them food, wine and other delicacies. However, the paper also reported on the same day that, in the village of Rethem, 15 British soldiers who had been taken prisoner by German troops, were stood up against a blazing wall and machine-gunned to death.

THESE ARE STILL THE GERMANS

3 May 1945
In Hitler's last will and testament, he had surprisingly chosen Grand Admiral Dönitz, Commander-in-Chief of the German Navy, as his successor as Head of State and Supreme Commander of the Armed Forces. Significantly, Dönitz was not to become Führer but President, a post Hitler had abolished years earlier. Hitler, whilst expelling both Hermann Göring and Heinrich Himmler from the Nazi Party for supposedly attempting to negotiate with the Allies behind his back, chose Propaganda Minister Joseph Goebbels as Head of Government and Chancellor of Germany. However on 1 May, unbeknown to Illingworth, Goebbels had committed suicide, the day after Hitler's death.

FIFTEEN MEN ON THE DEAD MAN'S CHEST

Night passes . . . and the Evil Things depart

WHODUNIT?

above

8 May 1945

This cartoon was published on Victory in Europe Day; the date when the Allies formally accepted the unconditional surrender of the armed forces of Nazi Germany and the end of Adolf Hitler's Third Reich. Illingworth is obviously still unaware of Goebbels's suicide.

22 May 1945

After the defeat of Germany, Winston Churchill proposed to the leader of the Labour Party, Clement Attlee that the war-time coalition should continue until victory had been achieved over Japan. However, when Attlee put this to the Labour Party Conference, opinion was hostile to a continuation of the coalition. Attlee wrote to Churchill to confirm that his Party would leave the coalition immediately. Churchill (under pressure from his Party to hold a quick election, to exploit his standing as the man who had won the war) then resigned as Prime Minister. This brought an end to the war-time coalition government.

5 June 1945
Churchill formed a caretaker government and announced that a general election would take place on 5 July. Labour's manifesto *Let Us Face the Future* set out comprehensive plans to 'win the peace' as their election posters put it. It proposed nationalisation of the Bank of England, fuel and power, inland transport and iron and steel. Planning would continue, with controls on raw materials and food prices, government intervention to maintain employment, a National Health Service and social security, and controls on the location of industry. On 4 June, Churchill made an election radio broadcast suggesting that Labour would ultimately need some kind of Gestapo to impose its socialist ideas and arguing that planning would lead to totalitarianism. Churchill stated:

> Look how even to-day they hunger for controls of every kind, as if these were delectable foods instead of war-time inflictions and monstrosities. There is to be one State to which all are to be obedient in every act of their lives.

WAKE UP GULLIVER

22 June 1945
Churchill had been an incredibly popular and successful war leader and few could imagine that the electorate would turn against him. Churchill made allegations that a Labour Government would be undemocratically controlled by the National Executive Committee of the Labour Party, and by its Chairman Harold Laski. Attlee, according to Churchill, would be little more than a puppet in Laski's hands. Laski had in the meantime issued libel writs on the *Nottingham Guardian* and the *Daily Express* for suggesting that he had said the following at an election rally in Newark, Nottinghamshire:

> If we cannot get the reforms we desire, we shall not hesitate to use violence, even if it means revolution.

THE FROGS WHO WOULD BE BULLS

THE LAST ENEMY

CHANGING THE BOWLING

above
15 August 1945
On the day this cartoon was published, Emperor Hirohito announced Japan's surrender over the radio. Some Japanese soldiers, devastated by the surrender, committed suicide; over 100 American prisoners of war were also executed. In addition, many Australian and British prisoners of war were illegally executed in Borneo by the Imperial Japanese Army, at both Ranau and Sandakan. Since Japan was the last Axis Power to surrender and V-J Day followed V-E Day by three months, V-J Day marked the official end of the war.

27 July 1945
Although the General Election was held on 5 July, the result was not declared until 26 July, due to the votes being collected in from those serving overseas. The result led to a landslide victory for the Labour Party. The election reflected the voters' belief that the Labour Party was better able to rebuild the country following the war than the Conservatives. Labour had also been given the opportunity during the war to display to the electorate their domestic competence in government under men such as Attlee, Morrison and Bevin at the Ministry of Labour. This was the first election in which Labour gained a majority of seats and also the first time it won a plurality of votes.

8 October 1945
President Truman repeatedly called for the British Government to allow 100,000 Jewish refugees, the approximate number of 'detained persons' in Europe at the time, into Palestine. Responding to Truman's pleas to admit more Jews, Prime Minister Clement Attlee proposed a joint commission to resolve the crisis. The Anglo-American Committee of Inquiry was established to review the issue of Jewish immigration to Palestine. The committee heard testimony from witnesses in Washington, London, Europe and the Middle East. Zionists demanded the immediate establishment of a Jewish Commonwealth in Palestine. Arabs, on the other hand, called for the establishment of an independent Arab state and an end to Jewish immigration, as well as a cessation of all land sales to Jews.

THE BILLETING OFFICER

22 October 1945
The Labour Government maintained most of the wartime controls over the economy by passing through the House of Commons a five-year economic controls Bill.

NO RELAXING ON THE TREADMILL

THE INCOMPLEAT ANGLERS

13 November 1945
Attlee met President Truman aboard the yacht *Sequoia* in Chesapeake Bay. The two leaders were concerned over the Soviet Union's territorial and political aims for the post-war world. Attlee suggested to Truman and his Secretary of State, James F Byrnes (seen here to the right of Attlee) his 'clear the air' plan for peace, whereby America should put all the secrets of the atom into a world-wide pool in return for the Soviets giving a definite guarantee and pledge to work and cooperate fully with the West.

CAUSE AND REFLECT

12 December 1945
When the war against Japan ended, the Americans abruptly cancelled, without prior warning, their Lend-Lease arrangement with Britain. The termination was so instantaneous and all-encompassing that ships leaving America bound for Britain with goods on board were refused permission to leave without payment up front. Britain badly needed money to pay for reconstruction and also to import food for a nation worn down after years of rationing. Britain was forced to enter into emergency negotiations to secure a £3.5 billion loan, the terms of which were not as favourable as had been hoped. Winston Churchill called the treatment by the Americans "rough and harsh".

31 January 1946
Coal was the second industry to be nationalised by the post-war Attlee government (after the Bank of England), the Coal Nationalisation Bill having been introduced at the end of 1945. The Minister of Fuel and Power, Manny Shinwell, alongsid Chancellor of the Exchequer, Hugh Dalton, is seen in the cartoon driving the nationalisation train to a dead end. However, Conservative opposition to coal nationalisation was in fact muted as there was widespread recognition that the industry needed support to survive. Interestingly, Illingworth has drawn the locomotive in the style of fellow cartoonist Roland Emett.

JOURNEY'S END

19 February 1946
Negotiations between the representatives of the wartime grand alliance, Attlee, Stalin and Truman, on the post-war peace were undermined by a growing sense of insecurity and mutual mistrust. Soviet spies had kept Stalin informed about the Americans' development of Atomic weapons, which helped the Russians develop their own by 1949.

GUNPOWDER, TREASON AND PLOT

THE CAUDILLO SEES RED

4 March 1946
On the day this cartoon was published, the three great post-war powers pledged to give aid to Spain on the condition that Franco stepped down. The ineffectual threat (Franco remained in power until his death in 1975) was triggered by Spain's 'non-belligerent' status during the war, although she provided support to the Axis powers, and the 'Blue Division', some 50,000 volunteers, had been sent to help German forces on the Eastern front. It was also a response to the programme of 'judicial executions' that had been going on since the Spanish Civil War ended in 1939.

PEEP UNDER THE IRON CURTAIN

6 March 1946
On 5 March, Churchill had been invited to accept an honorary degree in Fulton, Missouri. In a famous speech he warned that "an iron curtain" had been placed across Europe and that every Eastern European country behind this iron curtain had fallen or would soon fall under the Soviet Union's influence, both economically and militarily. The initial reaction to Churchill's speech was hostile. Stalin made a personal response, in which he accused the former Prime Minister of being "a firebrand of war" and compared his words to those of Hitler. Churchill's speech marked, for many, the beginning of the Cold War.

14 May 1946
Mahatma Ghandi was determined that once it had secured its independence from Britain, India should remain whole, despite the religious divisions within the country. However, the Moslem League, led by Mohammad Jinnah, called for partition and the creation of a Moslem state in what was to become Pakistan. Negotiations about the future shape of an independent India took place against a background of increasing religious strife.

JUNGLE POLITICS

Labour had been in office for one year.

8 July 1946
The euphoria that greeted the end of the war with Germany and Japan had now evaporated and British forces were still engaged in fighting in numerous trouble-spots around the world, including Palestine, Malaya, and India. At home, resource constraints were inhibiting the house-building programme (a quarter of the total housing stock having been destroyed or damaged during the war). Despite the fact that bread rationing had not taken place throughout the war it had been necessary to introduce it at the end of June 1946. Interestedly, the election poster in the top left hand corner of Illingworth's cartoon of the British soldier was drawn by the *Daily Mirror* cartoonist, Philip Zec.

FOOD FOR SECOND THOUGHTS...

THE REAL CASUALTY

23 July 1946
The King David Hotel was the British administrative and military headquarters in Palestine – it also served as the headquarters of the British Criminal Investigation Division. On 29 June, the British authorities carried out a raid on the Jewish Agency and confiscated a large number of documents. At the same time, approximately 2,500 Jews were arrested. Members of the Jewish underground military group, the Irgun, targeted the hotel both in revenge and as a way of destroying the documents. The leader of the Irgun, Menachem Begin, claimed that he saw the hotel solely as a military building and therefore a legitimate target. The bombing of the hotel on 22 July killed 91 people, including Jews who worked at the hotel. The explosion provoked outrage throughout the world, though Begin claimed that the British ignored warnings delivered the day before.

THE JUDGEMENT OF NUREMBURG

Guilty of 8 invasions

1 October 1946
On 30 September, the International Military Tribunal, which had been sitting in Nuremberg since 1945, gave judgment on 22 Nazi war criminals. Among others, Goering and von Ribbentrop were sentenced to death, while Hess was sentenced to life imprisonment.

7 January 1947
A combination of fuel shortages and one of the severest winters on record – in the very month that coal nationalisation came in to effect – created a crisis for the Attlee government. Manny Shinwell, minister for Fuel and Power, who was widely criticised for his failure to avert this crisis, is seen imposing the burden of fuel rationing on the nation.

THE LOADS THEY WANT TO SHED

A TIME FOR REFLECTION
'Hidden agenda'

17 March 1947
In January, General George C Marshall replaced James Byrnes as American Secretary of State and from 10 March attended the foreign ministers' conference in Moscow to finalise details of the post-war governments of Germany and Austria. However, because of Soviet intransigence and mutual suspicions between East and West, the conference failed to resolve any of the outstanding issues. On his return from Moscow, Marshall declared that "the patient is sinking while the doctors deliberate" and "at Moscow, propaganda appealed to passion and prejudice appeared to take the place of appeals to reason and understanding".

"I'LL KEEP THE SEAT WARM"

2 April 1947
The Spanish monarchy had been abolished since 1931 after the reigning King Alfonso fled the country. On 28 March, Franco presented the text for a proposed restoration of the monarchy, although he would remain as Head of State. This gesture was largely done to appease the monarchists. As a result, Franco did not allow the pretender, Juan de Borbón, Count of Barcelona, to take the throne.

21 May 1947
John Maynard Keynes had negotiated the detail of the United States loan to Britain (notionally worth $5 billion), shortly before his death in 1946. However by the summer of 1947 it became clear that the terms of the loan would reduce its value: Britain was committed to large-scale purchase from the United States, and the strength of the dollar in effect reduced the value of the loan. The Americans also insisted that the pound 'floated', becoming freely convertible – a disaster for the balance of payments given the strong dollar.

THE WATER-HOLE

The Paris "save Europe" talks were held in the Hall of Parrots.

3 July 1947
George Marshall had delivered a speech in June, inviting European countries including the Soviet Union to join in a co-operative plan for economic reconstruction. However, there were strings attached. The United States demanded explicit requirements for trade liberalisation and increases in productivity. The plan was seen from Moscow as an explicit attempt to lure Eastern European nations away from Communist influence and the Soviet Union withdrew from the talks on 2 July. Unlike the Molotov parrot, Foreign Ministers of Britain and France, Ernie Bevin and Georges Bidault, appear acquiescent.

BITING THE HAND...

'SAHIB! SAHIB!'

TWO-FOOT TROUBLE

above

28 August 1947

Independence from Britain was formally declared for Pakistan on 14 August and India on 15 August. Hindus left in the area allotted to Pakistan and Muslims who remained in India now began to fear for their lives as mobs in both countries attacked the new minorities. It is estimated that 1.5 million people were killed in the chaos. Partition as a result led to the largest transfer of population in history, with an estimated 14 million people leaving their homes for neighbouring Pakistan and India.

9 September 1947

Despite the coal industry passing into Government control as the industry was nationalised, a dispute in South Yorkshire about the length of seam to be mined in a shift and the subsequent strike by 45,000 miners led to the closure of steel works in Sheffield.

2 December 1947
Although the United Nations had assumed responsibility for Palestine, British troops were responsible for peace-keeping. On 1 December, the General Assembly of the United Nations voted by 33-13 to accept the idea of partitioning Palestine into two zones, one for the Jews (Israel) and the other for the Arabs (Palestine). Inevitably the new Israeli state was immediately criticised by the surrounding Arab nations, who walked out of the UN in protest.

SEPARATION ORDER

5 April 1948
In early 1948 the three western sectors of Berlin, which had been under the administration of Britain, France and the USA, were merged to create West Berlin. Stalin's response was to blockade the city in an attempt to force the Allies to leave Berlin. All rail and road routes going in and out of West Berlin through Soviet-controlled territory in Germany were closed. Military confrontation loomed.

PIN-PRICKS DUEL

30 June 1948
On 28 June, Stalin accused Marshall Tito of seeking favour with the West, and as a result expelled Yugoslavia from the Cominform. In order to bring the mutinous state and its leader into compliance with the Soviet Union, Stalin concocted an economic blockade, sedition, border incidents, and threats of military invasion, but these proved counter-productive as it only further united the Yugoslav people behind Tito.

BEVAN IN BLUNDERLAND

6 July 1948
In May, Bevan had given a speech in Manchester during which he had said "...no attempts at ethical or social seduction can eradicate from my heart a deep burning hatred for the Tory Party that inflicted those bitter experiences on me. So far as I am concerned they are lower than vermin." Illingworth sees this as contrasting with the Government's apparent attempt to woo Tory voters by increasing the sugar ration.

12 August 1948
The first Arab-Israeli war began on 15 May when the League of Arab States announced its 'intervention' against the state of Israel, which had been proclaimed hours before. The armies that attacked Israel were those of Syria, Lebanon, Iraq, Saudi Arabia, Egypt, and Jordan. For all their numerical superiority, the Arabs were ill-equipped, inexperienced and unprepared. By August, they had been defeated. Meanwhile, Israel grew beyond the partition lines, gained more defensible borders and by destroying Arab villages further reduced the Palestinian population.

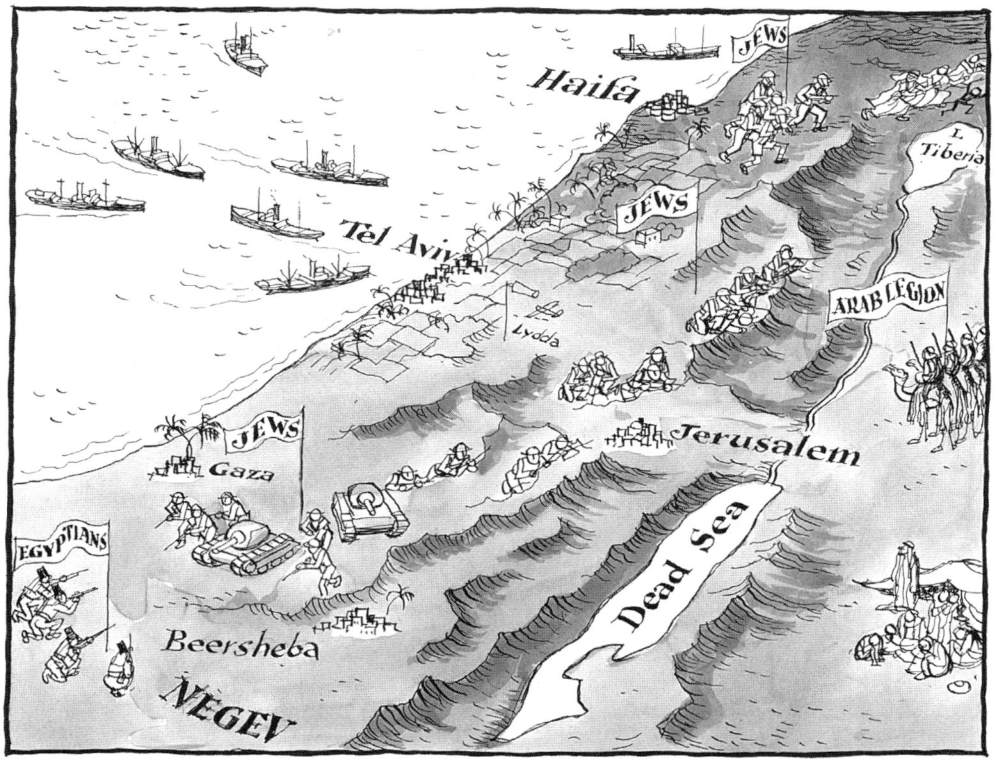

13 September 1948
On 30 January, Gandhi had been assassinated. On 11 September, Muhammad Ali Jinnah died at the age of 71. On the day this cartoon was published, Indian troops invaded the Muslim ruled state of Hyderabad, which had originally remained independent after the partition of India. It was later annexed by India. Earlier in the year, India and Pakistan had gone to war over Kashmir, which had had a Hindu ruler, but whose subjects were mostly Muslims. The fighting only ended when on 13 August the UN Security Council called for an immediate ceasefire and the withdrawal of all Pakistani and Indian troops and for the holding of a plebiscite under United Nations' supervision.

THE LOST LEADERS

8 YEAR'S AFTER...

15 September 1948
The Allied response to the Berlin blockade was to launch a massive airlift using both civil and military aircraft that flew supplies into West Berlin. This aerial supplying of West Berlin became known as the Berlin Airlift and it was estimated that over 2 million tonnes of supplies were delivered by almost 300,000 flights.

27 September 1948
The success of the Berlin Airlift was humiliating to the Soviets, who had repeatedly claimed it could never work. In August, the Soviet Governor in East Berlin attempted unsuccessfully to block the remaining air corridors in order to prevent the continuation of the airlift.

NO GO JOE!

4 November 1948
The presidential election of 1948 produced one of the biggest surprises in American electoral history. The Republican candidate, Thomas Dewey, was considered to be the firm favourite to defeat Truman. On election night, the *Chicago Tribune* even published an early edition with the headline 'Dewey defeats Truman'. Truman's victory, unsurprisingly, led to the overhaul of polling techniques in the United States.

LITTLE BRAT!

11 January 1949
The British Government complained bitterly to the American administration after the Israelis had shot down five British reconnaissance planes over Egypt. British Foreign Secretary, Ernie Bevin, told a Cabinet meeting that "it is impossible to get settlement over Israel with the United States and impossible to solve it without them".

7 February 1949
Cardinal Mindszenty's admissions of guilt before the People's Court in Budapest added to the long list of 'confessions' that marked the political trials in Eastern Europe for the previous 20 years - to the astonishment of the Western World.

SEEING THE LIGHT

THE SEED AND THE CROP

4 April 1949
The North Atlantic Treaty Organization (NATO) was signed in Washington on the day this cartoon was published. The treaty was a product of the containment policy developed by the West to stop the spread of Soviet Communism.

FOR THE DEFENCE

29 August 1949
A recession in America at the start of 1949 led to a growing dollar deficit. Under continuing economic pressure, and despite months of denials that it would do so, Sir Stafford Cripps, the Chancellor of the Exchequer, announced a 30% devaluation in the pound, from $4.03 to $2.80 in September.

26 September 1949
At the end of August the Soviet Union tested its first atomic bomb in the Kazakhstan desert, although Stalin issued no formal announcement. American scientists detected unusual radioactivity, and it was only confirmed by the Kremlin after Truman had announced the explosion had taken place on 23 September.

ATOM LANDSCAPE

17 November 1949
A General Election was expected shortly but the first skirmishes were triggered by a by-election in South Bradford that was held for Labour by George Craddock.

PRELIMINARY BOUT

THE SLEEPING BEAUTY

28 November 1949
The French Foreign Minister, Robert Schuman, was insistent that the dismantling of any German industry that could support rearmament should continue, despite growing German protests. In October, the British Foreign Secretary, Ernie Bevin, had written to Schuman saying that "the continuation of dismantling is causing great disquiet among the Labour Party here". Meanwhile, the US Secretary of State, Dean Acheson, was contemplating German rearmament as part of NATO defences against the Soviet Union.

THE ONE WHO GOT AWAY

1 December 1949
With a General Election imminent within the next year, the Conservatives were buoyed up by the news that after 14 years, the New Zealand Labour Government had been rejected by the electorate.

21 February 1950
Conscious that the outcome of the 1950 General Election, to be held two days after the publication of this cartoon, would be close, 'gaffe' prone Manny Shinwell was told to keep a low profile. The Tories continued to attack him, 'Shiver with Shinwell', for his failure to deal with the 1947 winter fuel shortage.

CONSPICUOUS BY HIS ABSENCE

27 February 1950
Although the 1950 General Election again failed to bring Churchill victory at the polls, the Labour Government's overall majority was reduced to five. Churchill took encouragement that the Conservative Party, with new enthusiasm and determination, could make the Government's life so intolerable, that it would soon be forced into calling a further election: "One more heave before the year is out," he wrote to a colleague, "I know I am going to be Prime Minster again. I know it."

DEPOSIT GUARANTEED

12 June 1950
Given the Government's tiny majority, both Labour and Tory competed for the support of Clement Davies, the Liberal leader. With Churchill's Liberal past and cavalier outlook on party, he was happy to contemplate an accommodation with the Liberals. Churchill saw the Conservatives as the true heirs to the Liberal vote, because according to him no true Liberal would vote for state control. The football world cup was taking place in Chile.

20 September 1950
In June, North Korean forces invaded South Korea. However, by September, a United Nations force launched an offensive that drove the North Koreans back across their own border.

25 September 1950
The Iron and Steel Nationalisation Act came into operation. Out of all the nationalisation programmes, the steel industry was the one that the Tories most stubbornly obstructed. "Were the Conservative Party to be returned to power," Churchill declared; "it would repeal the existing Iron and Steel Act irrespective of whether the vesting date had occurred or not."

THE NEW RECRUIT

STEALING THE LIMELIGHT

23 October 1950
Following Stafford Cripps' resignation on grounds of ill-health, Attlee appointed Hugh Gaitskell Chancellor of the Exchequer, in the face of opposition from the Left in the Party. Bevan, in particular, had used the Party Conference at Margate earlier that month to try to mend fences with Attlee.

It is announced that the Festival of Britain funfair is to have a Rotor machine in which people are kept suspended in a revolving drum by means of centrifugal force.

15 November 1950
The Rotor machine was described in the *Daily Mail* as the 'most up to date funfair attraction'. It was announced by the Food Minister that half a million fewer turkeys and geese would be available for this Christmas than last - and dearer too.

WAITING FOR THE FALL

6 December 1950
By November, United Nation forces under General Douglas MacArthur had crossed the 38th parallel, and had taken control of the greater part of Korea. However, this provoked the Chinese into intervening in Korea and resulted in Chinese forces halting the United Nations push against the North Koreans. Prior to the invasion, MacArthur had assured President Truman that China would not get involved, but he had been proved wrong.

STICKY WICKET

WILL THE AVALANCHE PASS?

27 December 1950
The Coronation Stone, the Stone of Scone, or the Stone of Destiny as it was variously called, was stolen in the early hours of Christmas Day from Westminster Abbey by four Scottish nationalists who took it back to Scotland. Four months later it was recovered and restored to the Abbey. The Stone of Scone was used to crown British monarchs up to and including Queen Elizabeth II.

24 January 1951
Despite America's determination to halt the Chinese advance into Korea through military means, 12 Asian and Arab States attempted to take a lead in seeking a peaceful settlement of the Korean conflict through the United Nations.

THE LIMPETS

top
5 March 1951
With Ernie Bevin's health deteriorating, Attlee found he had little choice but to remove him as Foreign Secretary. A heartbroken Bevin was instead given the position of Lord Privy Seal. "I am neither a Lord, nor a Privy, nor a Seal," he is said to have commented. He died the following month, still holding the key to his red box.

above
21 March 1951
Deputy Prime Minister, Herbert Morrison, in charge of putting on the Festival of Britain, had been forced to explain to MPs why another £1 million loan was required for the Festival Gardens at Battersea Park. Morrison told the House of Commons that he was "very cross about it". The extra costs were put down to 'an extraordinary loss of working time from incessant and continuing bad weather which kept the site in an extremely muddy state'. Morrison was advised that the only way to balance the budget of the Battersea Park Gardens was to make them a permanent feature of London life to which Morrison responded: "I think there will be a great agitation for the Gardens to be kept open permanently. And I want people to be happy. I want to hear people sing."

YOUR COIN WINS

9 April 1951
Hugh Gaitskell's first budget as Chancellor of the Exchequer included not only tax rises but also controversially the introduction of NHS charges for false teeth and spectacles. This was to help cover the costs of rearmament due to the war in Korea. Nye Bevan resigned from the Cabinet in protest apparently over the introduction of NHS charges, although the real catalyst was believed to have been his opposition to the Government's defence and foreign policy.

THE FLIGHT

The Brabazon, the world's largest airplane had its maiden passenger flight yesterday.

26 July 1951
Bevan's resignation split the Labour Party in two with those on the left of the Party (the Bevanites) and those on the right (the Gaitskellites). In a showdown with Bevan rebels, Attlee succeeded in getting the Labour Party executive to accept the need to carry out the Government's re-armament programme in full. It was now rumoured that Bevan would leave the Labour Party.

1 October 1951
In May, the newly-elected Persian leader, Dr Mohammed Moussadeq, who often did business in his pyjamas, had announced his decision to nationalise the country's oil industry. This meant the loss of Britain's largest single overseas investment, the Anglo-Iranian oil company. The British government reacted furiously. Clement Attlee imposed a naval blockade in the Gulf and asked the UN Security Council to condemn Iran. Instead, the Council embarrassingly came out in Iran's favour.

SHADES OF JOHN BULL

25 October 1951
In 1945, Labour's Attorney General, Sir Hartley Shawcross, is supposed to have said in the House of Commons, "We are the masters now." Five years later, on the day of the General Election that was to remove the post-war Labour Government from power, Illingworth amended the quotation. In fact, Shawcross had actually said, "We are the masters at the moment and shall be for some considerable time" in a debate to repeal the Conservatives' 'Trade Disputes Act' of 1927. Unusually for Illingworth, this cartoon was published on the front page of the *Daily Mail*.

"WE ARE ALL THE MASTERS NOW!"

THE PILOT GOES ABOARD AGAIN

27 October 1951
Despite receiving fewer votes than the Labour Party, the Conservatives won the 1951 General Election with an overall majority of 17. Winston Churchill became Prime Minister for the second time at the age of nearly 77. This made him the second oldest Prime Minister in history after Gladstone. This cartoon is an interesting reversal on Tenniel's original cartoon of Bismarck leaving office.

7 January 1952
On 5 January, Churchill arrived in the United States for his first official visit since being re-elected. He was there to discuss with President Truman how to respond to the Soviet Union's meddling in the Korean War. In the cartoon, the ears of Stalin and Foreign Minister Andrei Vishinsky are literally burning to find out what that their response will be.

10 July 1952
The Rev Hewlett Johnson, Dean of Canterbury Cathedral, was a Marxist and was widely known to contemporaries as "The Red Dean". After a trip to China, the Dean returned to Canterbury full of praise for the Communists and with what he said was "crushing evidence" that the Allies were conducting germ warfare in Korea. The evidence, shown to newsmen at a press conference, turned out to be a massive scroll written entirely in Chinese. The Dean was asked if he had seen anyone sick as a result of germ warfare. "Well, no," he said, "but I saw the brains of two children who had died from encephalitis, an unusual disease for this time of the year."

THE GERM

1 September 1952
Truman initially tried to moderate Churchill's stance towards Persia and the nationalisation of British oil interests, worried that outright British hostility would encourage Persia to turn towards the Soviets. However, Mossadeq's refusal to negotiate persuaded Truman a firmer line was needed. The following year Mossadeq was overthrown through joint Anglo-American action.

THE BORE

JILTED

RIDDLES FOR THE SPHINX

above
4 September 1952
At the TUC Conference at Margate, delegates overwhelmingly defeated two proposals attacking rearmament and also threw out a suggestion from the Shopworkers' Union, along Bevanite lines, that the arms drive should be scaled down to a level guaranteeing social services and living standards. The TUC General Secretary, Sir Vincent Tewson, appealed to the delegates to confirm the General Council's declaration supporting rearmament and "show a guiding light" to the rest of the world.

15 September 1952
The Egyptian Army, led by General Muhammad Neguib, forced Prime Minister Aly Maher out of office, following a bloodless coup. Maher had been slow to carry out social and land reforms demanded by the army. There were concerns in the West that the coup could lead to destabilisation elsewhere in the region.

LIMELIGHT

INFANT IN PERIL

22 September 1952
above
When Charlie Chaplin left New York for England to promote his film *Limelight*, the Director of the FBI, J Edgar Hoover, used the opportunity to persuade the United States Attorney to revoke Chaplin's re-entry permit. Chaplin was not an American citizen and had been accused by Hoover of 'un-American activities' and suspected him of being a Communist sympathiser. Chaplin opted instead to settle in Switzerland with his third wife, Oona O'Neill, the daughter of playwright Eugene O'Neill.

22 October 1952
On 21 October, British troops were flown to Kenya to deal with an insurgency by Kenyan rebels against the British colonial administration – the Mau Mau uprising. It did not succeed militarily, but it did cause considerable loss of life and it created a rift between the white settler community in Kenya and the Home Office in London. Kenyan independence followed in 1963.

above
23 November 1952
At the Labour Party annual conference at Morecambe, the Bevanites succeeded in winning six of the seven constituency party seats on the NEC. Attlee and Morrison reacted by introducing new rules banning all independent groups, such as the Bevanite group, within the Parliamentary Party.

STRANGE BACK-CLOTH

18 December 1952
In a Prague show trial ordered by Stalin, the General Secretary of the Communist Party of Czechoslovakia, Rudolf Slansky, and other senior Party members were tried on trumped-up charges of treason and espionage. The 11 defendants were found guilty and hanged in public. At the same time 156 Britons travelled as part of the British delegation to Vienna's Communist sponsored 'Peace Rally'. The delegation called for an immediate ceasefire in Korea as a prelude to new talks.

SOME ENTRANCE!

19 January 1953
On 20 January Eisenhower was sworn in as the 34th President of the United States, facing a series of foreign policy crises, including arrests in Berlin of former Nazis who were thought to be organising a plot to restore Nazi rule. On 13 January, Stalin was planning a new purge after *Pravda* and Radio Moscow announced that nine eminent doctors were under arrest and had confessed to murdering two Soviet leaders of the past.

What's in a name?

24 February 1953
After Germany's defeat, Alfried Krupps von Bohlen was tried as a war criminal and sentenced to imprisonment for 12 years. The Krupp industrial empire had been intimately tied to Nazi policies through the use of some 100,000 slave labourers from occupied Eastern Europe. In 1951 Krupps was released, and in February 1953 an Allied decree banned him from continuing work in the armaments trade, although he was to receive £55 million in compensation. These were the receipts from the sale of his assets in Krupps. However, as no one could be found to take over the firm, he regained control later that year.

12 March 1953
When Stalin died on 3 March, Georgy Malenkov replaced him as Soviet Premier and First Secretary of the Communist Party. Although not morbidly obese, Malenkov had a very full face that made him look heavier than he was, and Stalin sometimes ridiculed him for his weight. He was derisively nicknamed 'Malanya' (Melanie) due to his feminine, prominent hips.

THE NEW FACE and this is Illingworth drawing it

26 May 1953
The Coronation of Queen Elizabeth II was to be held in Westminster Abbey on 2 June. The Coronation route through London was designed by Sir Hugh Casson and according to the *Daily Mail*, 'the designs are swamped by the spirit of traditional jollity – the spirit of a genuine Festival of Britain – which runs to miles of bunting and tons of gilded cardboard'.

UNEASY SEAT

9 July 1953
In the wake of Stalin's death, expressions of dissent appeared in Poland and Hungary, while an uprising against Communist rule took place in East Germany.

THE NEXT STEP?

10 September 1953
On 7 September, Dr Konrad Adenauer was re-elected as Federal Chancellor of West Germany, with a strengthened mandate for both his policy of close co-operation with the West and for German re-unification. At a post-election rally, Adenauer called for "reunion – or rather liberation because Eastern Germany lives under slavery and in bondage".

GOOD-BYE GUY!

TWO-POWER CONFERENCE

4 November 1953
above
The Queen's Speech, delivered the day before this cartoon was published, had announced that: "My Ministers are consulting farmers and the trades concerned about new methods of providing price guarantees and of marketing which will be required as rationing and allocation cease to be necessary." Illingworth's interpretation was a little optimistic: rationing did not finally disappear for another year.

13 November 1953
Under pressure from Senator Joe McCarthy, the Eisenhower administration had been removing staff recruited under the previous Truman presidency, whom McCarthy had accused of being Communist sympathisers. By November 1953, he was attacking Eisenhower and had altered the "20 years of treason" catchphrase he had coined for the preceding Democratic administrations and began referring to "21 years of treason" to include Eisenhower's first year in office. Eisenhower was due to meet Churchill in Bermuda for talks on the subject of a possible summit meeting with the Soviets.

THAW? – WHAT THAW?

4 February 1954
The Berlin Conference was a meeting of the 'Big Four' foreign ministers: Dulles for the United States, Eden for Britain, Bidault for France and Molotov for the Soviet Union. Little progress was made, except with Austria, from which the Soviets agreed to withdraw if it were made neutral. The conference lasted for three weeks, but ended in deadlock.

HARK, HARK, THE WATCHDOG... BARK – BARK...

8 March 1954
President Eisenhower refused to take a public stand against Senator Joseph McCarthy's aggressive anti-communist campaign. As McCarthy became increasingly combative towards the Eisenhower Administration, Eisenhower faced repeated calls that he should confront McCarthy directly. Eisenhower refused, saying privately, "Nothing would please him [McCarthy] more than to get the publicity that would be generated by a public repudiation by the President." On several occasions Eisenhower is reported to have said of McCarthy that he did not want to "get down in the gutter with that guy."

10 March 1954
Since the overthrow of King Farouk in 1952, the British Government had been seeking Egyptian agreement to continue to allow a British military presence in the Suez Canal Zone. By the beginning of 1954, a struggle for power had developed in Egypt between General Nasser, President Neguib and Salahm Salem (seen fighting here), which made further negotiations impossible.

SOME OTHER TIME, PERHAPS?

Pointed comment on the inroads of Town on Country was made in a George Cruikshank etching of 1829 entitled 'London going out of Town' or 'The March of Bricks and Mortar'. Because it is as pertinent today as it was 125 years ago the cartoon is copied by Illingworth – with minor adaptation.

17 March 1954
After the war, it was decided that people and industry should be moved out of London to 'overspill' towns. In the 1950s, Swindon was designated as an overspill town with over 14,000 people having moved there from London since the end of the war.

MR CRUIKSHANK SAID IT IN 1829

EVERYTHING UNDER CONTROL

Professor Otto Frisch speaking of H Bomb tests said the explosion cannot get out of control.

29 March 1954

On 1 March, the United States tested the first hydrogen bomb in the Pacific archipelago of Bikini. The 15-megaton bomb was up to 1,000 times more powerful than the atomic bomb that destroyed Hiroshima and the explosion turned out to be so violent that it overwhelmed the measuring instruments, indicating that the bomb was much more powerful than the scientists had anticipated. One of the atolls was totally vaporised, disappearing into a gigantic mushroom cloud that spread at least 100 miles wide and dropping back to the sea in the form of radioactive fallout.

THE RED CARPET

22 April 1954

Evokiya Petrov's husband Vladimir, who ran the Soviet Union's spy operations in Australia, decided to defect. Soon afterward, the KGB decided to get Evokiya, who had not changed sides with Vladimir, back to Moscow. Russian couriers Karpinsky and Zharkov and the diplomat from the Russian Embassy in Canberra, Kistlitsyn, were ordered to escort Mrs Petrov back to Russia. However, after manhandling her onto a flight to Darwin, en route to Moscow, they were disarmed by Australian police. It was here that Mrs Petrov decided to seek political asylum in Australia so that she could remain in Australia with her husband.

FLYING VISIT

above
4 October 1954
Arsenal became the first English league team to play in Russia, when they travelled to play a friendly against Moscow Dynamo. They lost heavily.

6 July 1954
Jean Monnet, architect of the Common Market, was determined that there should be a European Defence Community, in which German rearmament would be possible only as part of the development of a federal Europe. The treaty was ratified by five of the original member states, but not by France because of Gaullist fears that the EDC threatened France's national sovereignty. As a consequence, the EDC was never established.

THE FRIGHTENED LADY

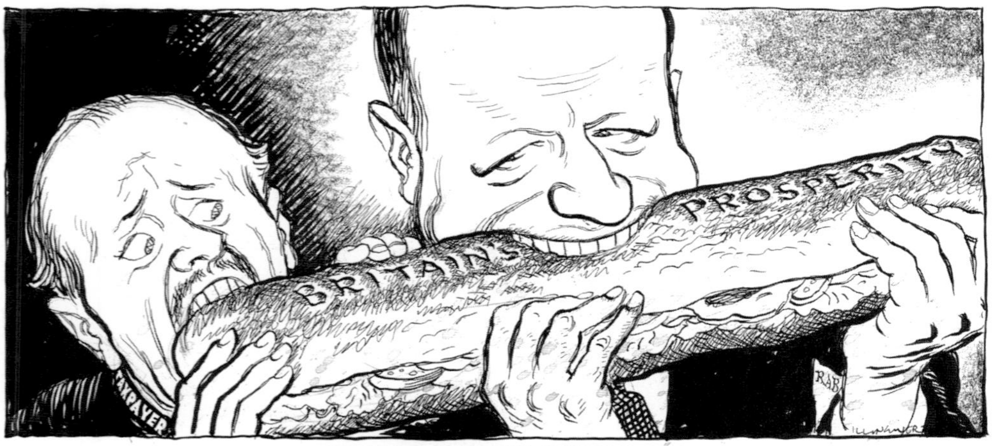

BIGGER BITE IN APRIL?

HERE IT IS! Britain's biggest submarine sandwich is launched with a mouthful for two

11 January 1955
Even after more than three years of a Conservative government the *Daily Mail* was still complaining about high taxes. However, Illingworth (correctly) anticipated a tax-cutting budget in April in anticipation of a General Election. In America, the latest eating craze was the three-foot submarine sandwich, as featured in the *Daily Mail* on the previous day.

21 April 1955
At the age of 80, Churchill resigned the office of Prime Minister.

29 April 1955
As expected, Anthony Eden became Prime Minister and called a General Election. Eden had plenty of reasons to be optimistic especially as the Labour Party was in disarray. For the election, Illingworth created 'Bevatskell' to symbolise the split in the Labour Party between those on the Right represented by Gaitskell and those on the Left represented by Bevan. This was also likely a play on the term 'Butskellism' which was used in reference to the political consensus associated with Butler and Gaitskell. The election campaign of 1955 was singularly uneventful. One journalist described its early stages as, 'the lull before the lull'.

FORWARD WITH BEVATSKELL

6 May 1955
On 6 May in Paris, Chancellor Dr Konrad Adenauer signed the official accession treaty which joined the Federal Republic of Germany to the North Atlantic Treaty Organisation. But there remained those who were suspicious of German rearmament and integration into European institutions, regularly expressing concerns about a Fourth Reich. At the signing Adenauer said:

> You will realise that this moment fills me with deep emotion. The German people have paid harshly for the horrors which were committed in their name by evil leadership and have paid for these horrors with unlimited suffering.

NO RESEMBLANCE WE HOPE

WILL THE SPARKLE LAST

6 July 1955
Nikita Khrushchev, who had by now replaced Malenkov as Soviet leader, prepared himself for the first summit meeting at Geneva to be held by the 'The Big Four' for ten years. The stated mission of the Geneva summit was to reduce tensions between East and West.

19 September 1955
President Perón was first elected President of Argentina in 1946. However, by 1955 he had become increasingly unpopular. Perón had also lost the leadership of a large part of the military which began to conspire against him. On 16 September, a military uprising deposed Perón and established a provisional government. Perón fled and sought asylum in Paraguay.

EL VAQUERO

"And I can now disclose, gentleman, that we have reason to believe that Queen Anne is deceased."

20 September 1955
Foreign Secretary, Harold Macmillan, finally admitted that British diplomats Guy Burgess and Donald Maclean, who had fled to Moscow in 1951, had been Russian spies for many years.

FOREIGN OFFICE RELEASE

THE KIND UNCLES

"Of course we'll give you a nice big loaded revolver for that scrap of paper."

30 September 1955
On 27 September, after Britain and America had refused to sell arms to Egypt, Colonel Nasser turned to the Soviet Union, which agreed to sell him $200 million worth of Soviet-made arms from Czechoslovakia. The Soviets also provided advisors to instruct the Egyptians in maintenance and operation of these armaments. The United States felt that the arms deal represented the most dramatic move yet in the Soviet campaign to increase its influence in the Middle East.

2 November 1955
On 31 October, Princess Margaret called off her plans to marry divorced Group Captain Peter Townsend. In a short statement, Princess Margaret said: "I have been aware that, subject to my renouncing my rights of succession, it might have been possible for me to contract a civil marriage." The second part of her statement is quoted by Illingworth in the cartoon itself on the steps to the throne. An almost identical cartoon by Illingworth, which later appeared in *Punch*, on Townsend's version of events published in the *Daily Mirror*, was given to the Queen after she requested it through the Duke of Norfolk. Illingworth expected "she wanted it as a joke."

24 January 1956
As inflation started to rise, the Cabinet attempted to bring down the cost of living by beginning an attack on monopolies and restrictive practices which they regarded as one of the key reasons for rising prices. Prime Minister Anthony Eden also singled out the importance of savings as a weapon against inflation.

THE KICK-OFF

Cast-Off

20 February 1956
In a speech at the Twentieth Congress of the Communist Party, Khrushchev shocked his audience by bitterly attacking Stalin's rule, exposing his excesses and mistakes and accusing him of 'flagrant abuses of power and brutality for the mass arrests [the purges] which caused tremendous harm to our country and to the cause of Socialist progress'. He said he wanted to break the 'Stalin cult' that had held Soviet citizens in its thrall for 30 years and gave orders for the Soviet Union's political prisoners to be released.

THE FINAL COURSE

14 May 1956
While on a goodwill visit to Britain, Soviet leaders Khrushchev and Bulganin, had been invited to a dinner organised by the Labour Party. During the meal, Khrushchev had an altercation with shadow cabinet minister, George Brown, and upon his return to the Soviet Union told *Pravda* that if he lived in Britain he would vote Conservative.

27 July 1956
Colonel Nasser announced that the Suez Canal would be nationalised in revenge for the United States and Britain withdrawing their offer to finance the construction of the Aswan Dam. Egypt, he said, would now use the revenue from the nationalised Suez Canal to build the dam. The announcement came after Nasser had been speaking for two hours and 20 minutes in Liberation Square, Alexandria, before an audience of 100,000. Obviously the Editor of the *Daily Mail* did not agree with Illingworth's assessment that Nasser was not a serious threat as he only published the left half of this cartoon in the paper.

NASSER HOLDS A GUN AT ALL OUR HEADS
This is what that canal means to you

30 July 1956
Because of Nasser's actions, supplies of fuel from the Middle East were blocked from going through the Suez Canal, causing fuel shortages in Britain. The Government soon suggested that petrol rationing may have to be introduced, much to the delight of black marketers.

HUNGARIAN RHAPSODY

29 October 1956
The Hungarian people attempted to overthrow the pro-Soviet regime in Budapest. Khrushchev took advantage of international disunity over the Suez Crisis, by sending 6,000 Russian tanks to Hungary. The uprising was crushed, and 30,000 Hungarians lost their lives.

UNDER FIRE

1 November 1956
Britain and France offered to temporarily occupy the Canal Zone and suggested a 10-mile buffer on either side, which would separate the Egyptian forces from the Israelis. Nasser refused, and on 31 October, Egypt was attacked and invaded by the military forces of Britain and France.

28 November 1956
The United States had made it clear that it was against any form of military action to resolve the Suez Crisis. President Eisenhower was furious after finding out that military action had taken place against Egypt by Britain, France and Israel. He made his anger known in public when he said, "We believe these actions to be taken in error." As a result, the United States increased economic pressure on the British government to remove its troops from the Canal Zone.

9 January 1957
Dr Edith Summerskill, Labour MP for Warrington, was criticised for visiting Egyptian wounded in Port Said hospitals instead of visiting British casualties. Summerskill wanted to see for herself the true position with regard to Egyptian casualties. Quoted in the *Daily Mail* on 8 February she said, "I was shocked at the evasion of the Government in giving the facts about the number of Egyptians killed and wounded in the Port Said landings."

VISITING DAY

10 January 1957
On 9 January, supposedly due to ill health, a humiliated Anthony Eden resigned as Prime Minister.

FORE!

20 February 1957
President Eisenhower was furious with the continued refusal of David Ben-Gurion, Israeli Prime Minister, to withdraw from the Sinai, which Israel had invaded as part of the British and French plan to take over the Suez Canal in November 1956. Eisenhower wanted "prompt and unconditional" withdrawal. Nasser's reaction to the Israeli occupation of Sinai was to refuse to clear the Suez Canal until total Israeli withdrawal had taken place. Eisenhower had a passion for golf and even had a putting green built outside the White House. He was often seen by passers by practicing his golf swing on the lawn.

10 May 1957
Despite protests from Japan and appeals from the Pope and Nehru, Prime Minister Harold Macmillan went ahead with exploding Britain's first hydrogen bomb at high altitude over the largely uninhabited Christmas Island on 15 May. The test raised a major debate about the dangers of nuclear weapons and led to the founding in 1958 of the Campaign for Nuclear Disarmament, which pressed for British and ultimately international, abandonment of nuclear weapons.

WHY PICK ON HIM?

As I was going up the stair, I saw a man who wasn't there. He wasn't there again today. I wish, I wish he'd go away.

16 May 1957
Lord Salisbury, seen here as a headless ghost, had resigned from the Government in March as Lord President of the Council over what he saw as the appeasement of Nasser. Salisbury now threatened to force a division unless the Government toughened its attitude towards the Egyptian leader. He told the House of Lords that the Government's position on Suez "comes far too near to a complete capitulation to Colonel Nasser than many of us would have felt palatable or, I was almost going to say, endurable."

24 May 1957
In 1956, Guy Mollett had formed a centre-left coalition government in France. Failures in dealing with the Algerian rebellion and the French economy led to that government's defeat, and Mollett's resignation, a year later.

21 October 1957
On the day this cartoon was published Macmillan left for Washington for talks with President Eisenhower on closer scientific and military co-operation between Britain and the United States.
Macmillan's earlier friendship with Eisenhower during the war helped in restoring the 'Special Relationship' between the United States and Britain that had been severely tested by the Suez Crisis debacle.

TOGETHER AGAIN?

9 December 1957
On 25 November, Eisenhower suffered a mild stroke. On 6 December, the world's media focused on the launch of America's latest rocket Vanguard TV-3 at Cape Canaveral. Live television carried the final minutes of the countdown. Although the engines ignited, the rocket only climbed four feet off the ground, before falling back onto the launch pad and collapsing in a massive fireball. A few days later, cleanup crews found the battered and burned satellite among the debris. "Most humiliating" was how Senator Lyndon B Johnson of Texas described the failure.

And the Carpenter said: "One side will make you grow taller and the other side will make you grow shorter."

6 January 1958
According to an article in the *Daily Mail*, "Mr Macmillan is fond of quoting *Alice in Wonderland* and like Alice his problem now is which side of the mushroom should he eat? After a year in office he is still the unknown Prime Minister." It also said that when Macmillan was Minister of Housing every memorandum that left his office carried a quotation from *Alice in Wonderland*.

10 March 1958
In Britain, a public debate took place over keeping the H-Bomb. J B Priestly came out publicly wanting Britain to "walk out of the nuclear arms race" and instead defend itself with conventional weapons. The *Daily Mail* believed that such attitudes were naïve in the extreme: "If the nations retain nuclear weapons they risk annihilating war. If they abandon them we British expose ourselves to submergence in the Communist world." The Oxford Union was about to debate the subject as they had in February 1933, when despite Hitler's rise to power, an Oxford Union resolution was passed stating that under no circumstances would the Union fight for King and Country.

14 March 1958
Having stepped back from his previous position of agreeing that Britain should keep the H-Bomb with the words, "It would mean sending a British Foreign Secretary naked into the United Nations Council Chamber", Bevan, according to the *Daily Mail*, was about to recant and once again join those who wanted to 'ban-the-bomb'. Under the heading, Gaitskell faces battle bid for power by H-Bomb switch, a *Daily Mail* article stated: "At the van of an army with such a powerful cause, so the group argues, Mr Bevan could sweep his implacable rival [Gaitskell] off the board and take over the leadership."

IT'S THAT MAN AGAIN

7 April 1958
On the day this cartoon was published 3,000 anti-H bomb demonstrators arrived at Aldermaston after a three-day march from London. Twelve thousand supporters of the new Campaign for Nuclear Disarmament then attended the final rally at the gates of the Atomic Weapons Research Establishment at Aldermaston.

"They're quite right you know. Before the H bomb we ALWAYS had good weather at Easter."

WHO LAUGHS LAST?

23 April 1958
As crowds protested outside the Governor's Palace, Maltese Prime Minister Dom Mintoff resigned. He did this in protest against the British terms for the future of Malta, especially Britain's decision to cut Malta's allowance by £1 million and her policy on integration with Britain. Mintoff stated:

> The hour of our trial has arrived. The Maltese people, who in the past have fought so many battles for other people, now have the chance to prove to the world they have grown into a nation.

Illingworth obviously believed that the ungrateful Maltese had short memories. Malta had been awarded the George Cross by King George VI after being battered by the German Luftwaffe during the war.

16 May 1958
During a goodwill trip through Latin America, Vice President Richard Nixon's limousine was attacked by an angry crowd and nearly overturned while travelling through Caracas, Venezuela. The incident was the dramatic highlight of a trip characterised by Latin American anger over some of America's Cold War policies. On the same day as the attack on Nixon, violent anti-American protests erupted in Algeria, Burma and Lebanon. A distraught Eisenhower told his secretary, "I am about ready to go put my uniform on."

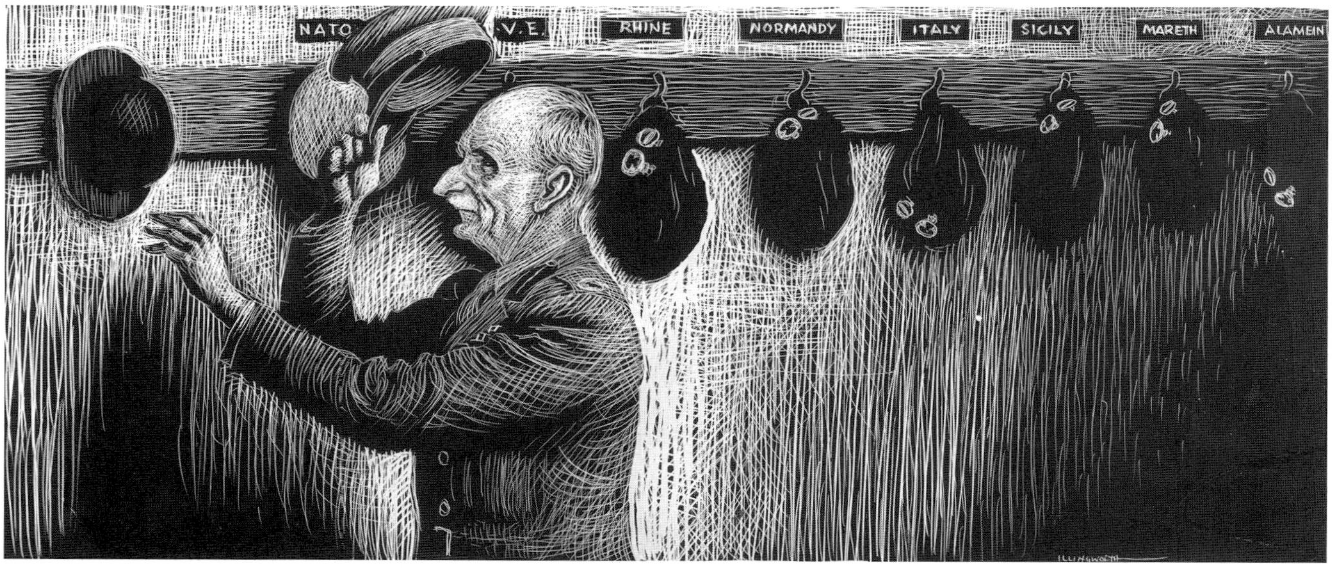

18 September 1958
On 17 September, 1st Viscount Montgomery of Alamein retired aged 71, relinquishing his post as Deputy Supreme Allied Commander in Europe.

29 October 1958
In 1956, Boris Pasternak had completed his masterpiece, Doctor Zhivago. The novel was refused publication as the authorities thought it anti-Communist, but the manuscript was smuggled into Italy where it was published to international acclaim. On 23 October 1958, Pasternak was awarded the Nobel Prize for literature. The Soviet regime was outraged. Pasternak was persecuted and despite turning down the Nobel Prize, he was officially witch-hunted and threatened with expulsion by Khrushchev.

THE BURNING OF THE BOOKS

THE LAST STAGE IN ORBIT

28 January 1959
In 1958 Khrushchev, having expelled Malenkov and Molotov from the Communist Party, was now the undisputed leader of the Soviet Union. He promoted reform of the Soviet system and began to place an emphasis on the production of consumer goods rather than on heavy industry. In a speech to the 21st Congress of the Communist Party, Khrushchev promised Russians less work, more food and a tax-free future in which they would beat the West in peaceful competition. He also reminded the West that Russia had the lead in the production of intercontinental missiles and could now send rockets "to any part of the globe without a miss".

"Thank you... we'll take over now."

13 February 1959
After four years a bloody guerrilla campaign in Cyprus by EOKA (National Organization of Cypriot Fighters) against British colonial rule came to an end on 19 February. The London Agreement signed by British, Greek, Turkish and Cypriot leaders guaranteed independence for Cyprus.

23 February 1959
Macmillan visited Moscow for talks with Khrushchev and attracted the media's attention by wearing a white Finnish lambswool shapka that he had bought in Russia 30 years earlier.

30 March 1959
below
At the beginning of March an anti-Chinese and anti-Communist revolt erupted in Lhasa, the capital of Tibet. This had been under the reign of the Chinese since 1950. It is estimated that 86,000 Tibetans died in the events surrounding the 1959 uprising. Members of the Dalai Lama's bodyguard remaining in Lhasa were disarmed and publicly executed, along with Tibetans found to be harbouring weapons in their homes. Thousands of Tibetan monks were also executed or arrested, and monasteries and temples around the city were looted or destroyed. The *Daily Mail* referred to Tibet as the Hungary of the East and stated:

> The mind goes back to 1956, when the Hungarians were treated in a similar fashion at the hands of the Red Army. Mr Khrushchev has recently been trying very hard to remove the black spot of Hungary from all memories. It must be aggravating for him to have the tragedy which shocked the Western Hemisphere re-enacted for the benefit of the East.

Now, Election Snakes and Ladders, the 'party' game with a difference

PLAY AS YOU WAIT

for results tonight

HERE is a party-political game, a game YOU can REALLY PLAY. Play it, and let your polling night party go with a swing. Play it, and dispel the tension of waiting for marginal results.

The rules are simple.

1. This is a game for 2, 3 or 4 players, each player having previously decided whether he plays as a Conservative or as a Labourite. (All right, you can swap next time. And apologies to Liberals who must temporarily forswear Party allegiance.)
2. Starting at space 1, the players move their counters (use coins) along the squares according to the value shown by the throw of a dice. (No dice? Make one out of a piece of cork.) A six entitles another throw.
3. Conservatives are affected only by Conservative snakes and ladders, shown in white on the board. Labour players are affected only by Labour snakes and ladders, shown in black. Snakes and ladders belonging to the other side are to be ignored.
4. Players alighting on the head of one of their snakes must take a downward course to its tail and proceed from there. Players alighting at the foot of one of their ladders ascend smartly to the top and proceed from there.
5. You must throw the exact number required to win. If you throw more than you need you must go up to the end and then move backwards an amount of squares equivalent to the excess.
6. Striped Don't-Know snake on square 99 affects both Conservative and Labour players. Land here and down you go, irrespective of Party.
7. First man through the door of Number 10, Downing-street is the winner.
8. No mud-slinging.

Now carry on and play the game.

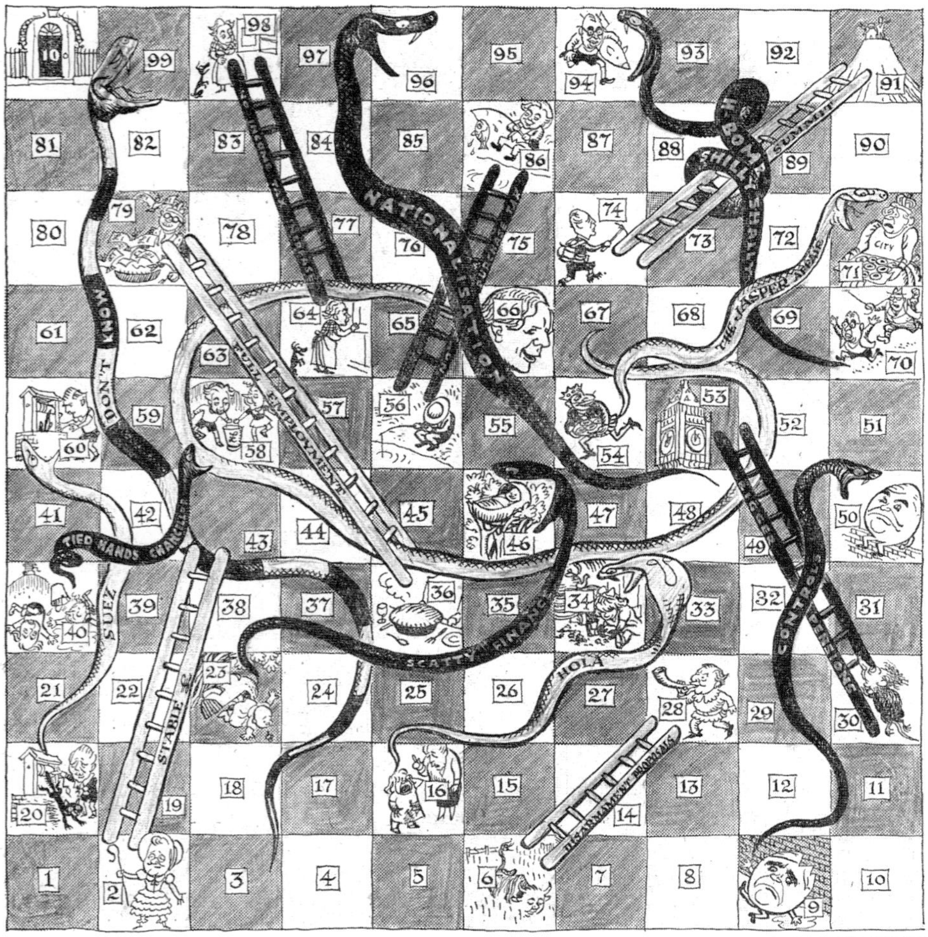

By ILLINGWORTH

8 October 1959

This cartoon was published on the day of the 1959 General Election. It resulted in a third successive victory for the ruling Conservative Party, led by Macmillan. The Conservatives even increased their overall majority to 100 seats over the Labour Party.

12 November 1959
Foreign Secretary Selwyn Lloyd embarked on the task set for him by Macmillan of mending Britain's relations with Europe and especially with France. Lloyd's main task was to create a 'bridge' between the Common Market Six and the Outer Seven of which Britain was a member.

DRIFTING APART

30 December 1959
In West Germany, members of the extreme right wing D.R.P Party were arrested after the Christmas Eve desecration of a Cologne Synagogue that had been daubed with swastikas and the Nazi slogan "Jews get out". The affair aroused a wave of sympathy for West Germany's 35,000 Jews. German Chancellor Dr Adenauer sent a telegram to the Jewish community in Cologne expressing his "revulsion" at this "atrocious deed".

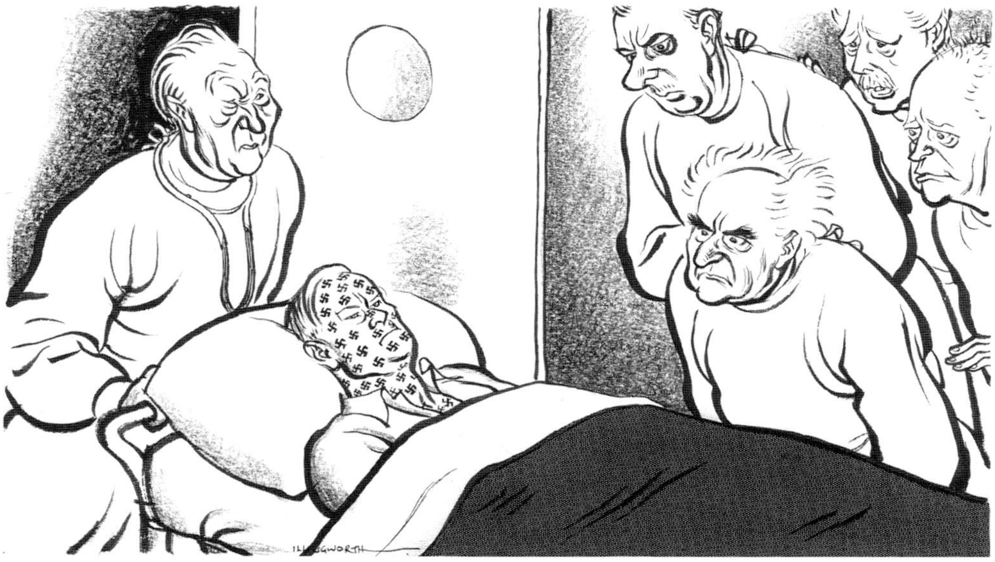

MEASLES AGAIN

30 November 1959
After losing three elections in a row, Gaitskell came to believe that public opposition to nationalisation had led to the Party's poor performance, and announced that he proposed to amend Clause IV (on public ownership) from the Labour Party Constitution. This, however, proved unpopular with the Party and Clause IV remained in the Constitution.

THE GAP

THE CASUALTY

top
27 January 1960
Shadow Foreign Secretary Nye Bevan had gone into hospital for a major abdominal operation on 29 December 1959. By the time this cartoon was published, it was found that he was in need of 'prolonged convalescence' and thus unable to return to his duties in the House of Commons. Gaitskell appointed Denis Healey to cover for Bevan in the House until he had recovered. However, Bevan was terminally ill with cancer, and died six months later on 6 July.

bottom
1 April 1960
In South Africa, the pass laws required all black men and women to carry personal documentation and stipulated that anyone found in a public place without their pass could be arrested and detained for up to 30 days. On 21 March, a crowd protesting against the pass laws gathered outside the police station in Sharpeville, a black township 28 miles southwest of Johannesburg. The police opened fire and 69 demonstrators were killed, including women and children.

A wave of strikes and street protests followed the Sharpeville massacre and on 30 March the South African Government declared a state of emergency. Both the African National Congress and the Pan-African Congress, the major vehicles for black political activism, were banned and forced underground or into exile.

"FATHER I CANNOT TELL A LIE..."

9 May 1960
On 1 May an American U2 spy plane was shot down over Russia. The US State Department at first claimed that it was simply an aircraft that had gone astray. Then, when Khrushchev produced photos taken by the pilot of military installations, President Eisenhower admitted he had authorised the flight but refused to apologise.

THE SUFFRAGETTE OF ATOM CORNER

1 June 1960
The General Secretary of the Transport and General Workers' Union and one of CND's founder members, Frank Cousins, made good his challenge against Gaitskell, an opponent of unilateralism, at the October 1960 Labour Party Conference in Scarborough. Wielding the union's bloc vote Cousins pushed through a resolution committing the Party to unilateral nuclear disarmament. The cartoon is reminiscent of when Emily Wilding Davison threw herself under the King's horse at the 1913 Derby.

18 May 1960
Without an apology from Eisenhower over the U-2 spy plane incident, Khrushchev walked out of the 'Big Four' East-West summit that was held in Paris and also attended by Eisenhower, Macmillan and de Gaulle. According to the *Daily Mail*, Soviet Defence Minister, Marshal Rodion Malinovsky's presence at the summit 'had strengthened fears that the icebergs of the cold war may drift back into East-West relations with a menace unknown since the death of Stalin seven years ago'.

GREAT EXPECTATIONS

10 June 1960
According to the *Daily Mail*, Hugh Gaitskell would resign his leadership after the annual conference at Scarborough in October if he was defeated on his defence policy. Despite defeat he did not resign and responded with his famous 'fight and fight and fight again' speech, which rallied Labour supporters of NATO and saw CND defeated at the 1961 Conference. This rather morbid cartoon seems now in rather bad taste considering Hugh Gaitskell died on 18 January 1963 at the age of 56.

THREE MORE FOR ADOPTION

24 June 1960
Following a period of stable economic growth various pressures began to impinge on Macmillan's Government. Inflation and stagnation began to characterise the economy as the Government struggled to control money supply, narrow the trade gap and restore gold reserves. Defence spending was high as Macmillan wanted Britain to develop its own independent nuclear deterrent. Realising that Britain was too reliant on trade with Commonwealth countries, Macmillan sought to build up trade links with Europe and played a leading role in the foundation of the European Free Trade Association (EFTA). EFTA sought closer union with the 'inner six' members of the European Economic Community (EEC), but this approach was unpopular with some sections of the Conservative Party.

14 November 1960
On 11 November John F Kennedy defeated Richard Nixon (seen here in the wings) in the 1960 presidential election, becoming the youngest person ever elected to that office. This is a strange and another rather prophetic cartoon as Kennedy and Monroe had never met. Two years later on 19 May 1962, Marylyn Monroe sang 'Happy Birthday, Mr President' at a celebration for Kennedy's 45th birthday. It was said by this time that Monroe and Kennedy were having an affair. The reason she appears in this cartoon is that, coincidentally on the day of Kennedy's election victory, it was announced that Monroe and playwright Arthur Miller were to divorce.

THE NEW ARRIVAL

24 February 1961
Adolf Eichmann, the SS officer who had been dubbed the 'Chief Executioner of the Third Reich' for his involvement in the Holocaust, had fled Europe in 1947 and settled in Buenos Aires. The Israeli Secret Service (Mossad) eventually tracked him down, however, and on 21 May 1960 kidnapped him, flying him to Israel to stand trial for crimes against humanity.

12 April 1961
On 11 April, Eichmann facing 15 charges, including crimes against humanity, crimes against the Jewish people and war crimes, went on trial in Jerusalem. He was found guilty and hanged on 1 June 1962.

LINE OF SUCCESSION

17 April 1961
On 12 April, Yuri Gagarin became the first human to enter space and orbit the earth. Since the mid-1950s Britain had witnessed the emergence of various youth subcultures. The earliest of these were the so-called Teddy Boys. These first teenagers were visible not only on account of their 'Edwardian' costumes but also their delinquent and sometimes violent behaviour. They were proud of belonging to the English working class, and reacted aggressively to the influx of West Indians, whom they saw as a threat to their already disintegrating working-class communities.

21 April 1961
Cuba had been viewed as a thorn in the side of the US since Castro's guerrillas had taken power in 1959. In April 1961 Kennedy backed an attempt by Cuban exiles to oust Castro and his Marxist regime, but the attempted invasion via the Bay of Pigs was a fiasco, driving Castro closer to the Soviet Union and strengthening the view of Nikita Khrushchev that Kennedy was a weak and inexperienced leader.

THE FIRST TEST

THE AWAKENING
'And what a big pipe you're smoking Gran'ma...'

7 June 1961
above
On 4 June, Khrushchev and Kennedy met for the first time in Vienna. Khrushchev threatened Kennedy that he would sign a separate peace treaty with East Germany, effectively cutting off Allied access to West Berlin. Kennedy was startled by Khrushchev's combative style and tone and unsettled by the Soviet premier's threat.

4 September 1961
From November 1958 until September 1961 the United States and the Soviet Union observed a moratorium on testing nuclear weapons. As Cold War tensions increased this informal truce began to collapse. The Soviet Union resumed testing of nuclear weapons and prepared to detonate 'Tsar', a device of 58 megatons, nearly 4,000 times more powerful than the bomb dropped on Hiroshima in 1945.

27 October 1961
One particular crossing point between East and West Berlin, Checkpoint Charlie, gained worldwide notoriety in October when American and Soviet tanks confronted each across the divide. The stand-off ended peacefully 16 hours later when Kennedy and Khrushchev agreed to pull back their forces.

THE NEXT MOVE

3 November 1961
After the war, Britain experienced labour shortages, especially in the transport sector and the National Health Service. Many of these jobs were taken by people from Commonwealth countries such as Jamaica, Pakistan and India. However, there was strong prejudice against non-white immigrants who were often refused accommodation and abused and attacked in the street. The 1961 Commonwealth Immigration Act restricted the number of people allowed to enter Britain from the former colonies. As most ex-colonies were in Africa, Asia and the West Indies the act was widely seen as imposing a 'colour bar', designed to exclude only non-white immigrants.

NO ROOM AT THE INN

LATE ENTRY

8 November 1961
Britain's first attempt to join the Common Market in 1957 was negotiated by Edward Heath, as Lord Privy Seal. German Chancellor Konrad Adenauer and French President Charles De Gaulle were both suspicious of British intentions.
The beauty pageant theme might have been chosen by Illingworth as Rosemarie Frankland was crowned Miss World in 1961, the first Briton to win the title.

THE LIBERALS ARE THE FACELESS MEN OF POLITICS – Iain Macleod

26 March 1962
The Liberal Party won the Orpington by-election from the Conservatives with an enormous swing of 26.8%. The result gave rise to the political phenomenon 'Orpington Man', who symbolised the rebellion of traditional Tory voters against the Macmillan Government. It is still regarded as one of the biggest by-election upsets in British political history.

22 April 1964
Both the United States and the Soviets proposed cuts in the production of nuclear weapons. The most visible achievements on arms control by the superpowers were the conclusion of the Outer Space Treaty (1967) and the Nuclear Non-Proliferation Treaty (1968).

Slow Strip

27 May 1964
On 13 March 1946, David Low had created the TUC Carthorse to symbolise the trade unions. This representation is still popular today with British cartoonists.

THE FIRST TEST

THE AWAKENING
'And what a big pipe you're smoking Gran'ma...'

7 June 1961
above
On 4 June, Khrushchev and Kennedy met for the first time in Vienna. Khrushchev threatened Kennedy that he would sign a separate peace treaty with East Germany, effectively cutting off Allied access to West Berlin. Kennedy was startled by Khrushchev's combative style and tone and unsettled by the Soviet premier's threat.

4 September 1961
From November 1958 until September 1961 the United States and the Soviet Union observed a moratorium on testing nuclear weapons. As Cold War tensions increased this informal truce began to collapse. The Soviet Union resumed testing of nuclear weapons and prepared to detonate 'Tsar', a device of 58 megatons, nearly 4,000 times more powerful than the bomb dropped on Hiroshima in 1945.

27 October 1961
One particular crossing point between East and West Berlin, Checkpoint Charlie, gained worldwide notoriety in October when American and Soviet tanks confronted each across the divide. The stand-off ended peacefully 16 hours later when Kennedy and Khrushchev agreed to pull back their forces.

THE NEXT MOVE

3 November 1961
After the war, Britain experienced labour shortages, especially in the transport sector and the National Health Service. Many of these jobs were taken by people from Commonwealth countries such as Jamaica, Pakistan and India. However, there was strong prejudice against non-white immigrants who were often refused accommodation and abused and attacked in the street. The 1961 Commonwealth Immigration Act restricted the number of people allowed to enter Britain from the former colonies. As most ex-colonies were in Africa, Asia and the West Indies the act was widely seen as imposing a 'colour bar', designed to exclude only non-white immigrants.

NO ROOM AT THE INN

LATE ENTRY

8 November 1961
Britain's first attempt to join the Common Market in 1957 was negotiated by Edward Heath, as Lord Privy Seal. German Chancellor Konrad Adenauer and French President Charles De Gaulle were both suspicious of British intentions.
The beauty pageant theme might have been chosen by Illingworth as Rosemarie Frankland was crowned Miss World in 1961, the first Briton to win the title.

THE LIBERALS ARE THE FACELESS MEN OF POLITICS – Iain Macleod

26 March 1962
The Liberal Party won the Orpington by-election from the Conservatives with an enormous swing of 26.8%. The result gave rise to the political phenomenon 'Orpington Man', who symbolised the rebellion of traditional Tory voters against the Macmillan Government. It is still regarded as one of the biggest by-election upsets in British political history.

22 January 1962
The Organisation de l'Armée Secrète (OAS) was a short-lived French right-wing terrorist group formed in February 1961 to resist the granting of independence to the French colony of Algeria. The OAS was created in response to the referendums on self-determination for Algeria. The OAS even attempted to assassinate Charles de Gaulle in January in an ambush at Petit-Clamart, a Paris suburb.

WINTER GALES

KEY QUESTION

above
23 May 1962
Chairman Mao's 'Great Leap Forward'; the attempt to collectivise agriculture throughout Communist China ended in a famine that starved at least 30 million people to death. The Communist Government attempted to conceal the catastrophe from the outside world, abetted by the few Western visitors to the country, such as France's Mitterand, who declared there was no famine. The Communist Party leadership knew the truth but couldn't acknowledge the widespread starvation until Mao did so himself.

30 July 1962
Britain's negotiating team headed by Edward Heath ran into difficulties when neither Britain nor the six countries of the EEC would budge from their positions on the subject of the temperate agricultural exports from the Commonwealth. The atmosphere, according to the *Daily Mail*, appeared to be one of 'total deadlock'.

16 August 1962
At 87, Churchill broke his left thigh in a serious fall at the Hotel de Paris in Monte Carlo. With his leg in plaster he was flown back to London where he underwent an operation to set the bone. Churchill remained in hospital for five more weeks while his own residence at Hyde Park Gate was altered so that he could live on the ground floor. Macmillan paid Churchill a visit and discussed with him Britain's bid to enter the European Common Market. This was not to Sir Winston's liking. Although he saw a need for a united Europe, he had no intention of including Britain. "Britain," he said, "should be with it though they could not be of it." General Montgomery was an unfailing friend and companion to Churchill in his last few difficult and debilitating years. But on one occasion after a hospital visit, Montgomery announced that Sir Winston was against going into the Common Market. Sir Winston was said to have been furious with Monty's indiscretion, which he labelled as 'monstrous'.

20 August 1962
On 17 August, Peter Fechter, an 18 year old East Berliner, bled to death at the base of a barricade after being shot multiple times by East German border guards during the course of an escape attempt across the Berlin Wall. For the West German public, Fechter's death brought home with unprecedented directness the barbarity of the shoot-to-kill order in effect along the inner-German border. Russian cosmonauts Major Nikolayev and Lt-Col Popovich, had orbited the earth on the first anniversary of the Berlin Wall in separate spacecraft.

"OK MR PRESIDENT, LET'S TALK."

29 October 1962
As the Cuban Missile Crisis intensified, President Kennedy declared a naval blockade of Cuba and threatened the Soviet Union with attack if any Cuban missile were ever launched against any country. With further Russian ships already on their way to Cuba and apparently prepared to ignore the blockade, nuclear war started to seem a real possibility. Khrushchev eventually backed down on 28 October, ordering Soviet vessels to turn back and agreeing to dismantle all Soviet missiles based in Cuba and ship them back to the Soviet Union.

THE WINDOW SHOPPERS

19 December 1962
Tony Benn was elected to the House of Commons in 1950. In 1960, his father, Lord Stansgate, died and Benn inherited his title, automatically losing his seat in the Commons. Benn campaigned for a change in the law so that peers could be allowed to renounce their titles. In 1963, the Conservative Government agreed to introduce the Peerage Bill allowing individuals to disclaim peerages. The timing of the Act had a significant influence on British politics as it was rumoured that Macmillan would soon retire as Prime Minister. In this prophetic cartoon, Illingworth shows that Lords Hailsham, Hinchingbrooke and Home are considering renouncing their peerages so that they will be eligible to stand in a future leadership contest.

"WHERE NOW?"

above
16 January 1963
On 14 January, General de Gaulle (described by the Foreign Office as an 'almost impossible ally') brutally vetoed Britain's bid to join the Common Market. It was a blow that delayed Britain's entry for a decade and hastened the end of Harold Macmillan's political career.

15 February 1963
Gaitskell died suddenly on 18 January sparking off a leadership contest within the Labour Party. On 14 February, Harold Wilson was elected Labour leader, and set about creating the image of a modern, dynamic Party, keen on utilising what he called 'the white heat of the technological revolution' to boost Britain's prosperity.

THE NEW DOLL

THE VOLCANO

7 May 1963
After black protests and demonstrations in South Africa over the Sharpeville massacre, South African Prime Minister, Dr Hendrik Verwoerd (seen here) declared a state of emergency, giving security forces the right to detain people without trial.
Over 18,000 demonstrators were arrested, including much of the ANC leadership, and the organisation was banned.
As activists continued to be arrested, the ANC began a campaign of sabotage.
In America, Martin Luther King led non-violent demonstrations in Birmingham, Alabama in order to confront the system of segregation. King reasoned that the response of the police would be to suppress the demonstrations violently, which, most likely, would attract national attention and create public sympathy for the cause of desegregation. King reasoned correctly. The response was as expected with police dogs and fire hoses used to disperse the demonstrators.
On 30 April, in Bristol, England, local West Indian activists publicly exposed the Bristol Bus Company's long standing colour bar against black bus crews. The bar was perfectly legal, for although an Immigration Act had been passed the year before, no law yet existed against racial segregation or discrimination.
The Passenger Group of the TGW Union in Bristol reportedly passed a resolution in January that coloured workers should not be employed as bus crews.

3 July 1963

The 12-year-old spy mystery of who was the Third Man was solved when it was revealed that it had been ex-diplomat Kim Philby. He had just been spotted in the Soviet Union for the first time since his disappearance in January. It was Philby who had tipped off the two Foreign Office diplomats Burgess and MacLean that the security services were onto them and so enabled them to flee to Russia in May 1951. In November 1979, Prime Minister Margaret Thatcher named Sir Anthony Blunt, a former security service officer and personal adviser on art to the Queen, as the 'Fourth Man' in the Cambridge spy ring.

'Oh, no, sir... we're <u>positive</u> there isn't a Fourth Man!'

25 September 1963

The Denning report said that Macmillan and his Ministers had failed in their handling of the Profumo affair. Although security had not been endangered they had not dealt with the ex-War Minister's relationship with a call girl even when it was affecting public confidence. Hundreds of people scrambled for the first copies of the report when it went on sale in London shortly after midnight. The Opposition, led by Harold Wilson, benefited greatly from the Government's embarrassment.

16 October 1963
Macmillan suddenly resigned as Prime Minister when diagnosed with prostate cancer from which he was not expected to recover (an incorrect diagnosis, as it turned out). At the time, the Conservative Party had no formal procedure for selecting a leader, and as would-be candidates made their ambitions known at the annual Party Conference, four front-runners appeared: Rab Butler, Reginald Maudling, Lord Hailsham and Lord Home. To many people's surprise, Macmillan suggested to the Queen that Home should succeed him.

21 October 1963
Before assuming the premiership, Lord Home renounced his hereditary title, becoming Sir Alec Douglas-Home. Iain Macleod and Enoch Powell, who had strongly opposed the candidacy of Home, refused to serve in the Cabinet under him as Prime Minister. This refusal was not based on antipathy to Home personally but was in protest against what Macleod and Powell saw as Macmillan's underhand manipulation of colleagues during the process of choosing a new leader.

25 November 1963
On 22 November President Kennedy was assassinated by Lee Harvey Oswald in Dallas, Texas. Kennedy was synonymous with his rocking chair, which helped to ease his back pain and was so attached to it that his aides would bring it aboard Air Force One whenever he travelled around the United States or the world. Kennedy bought more rocking chairs for Camp David as well as the Kennedy estates, which were located in Hyannis Port, Massachusetts, and Palm Beach, Florida.

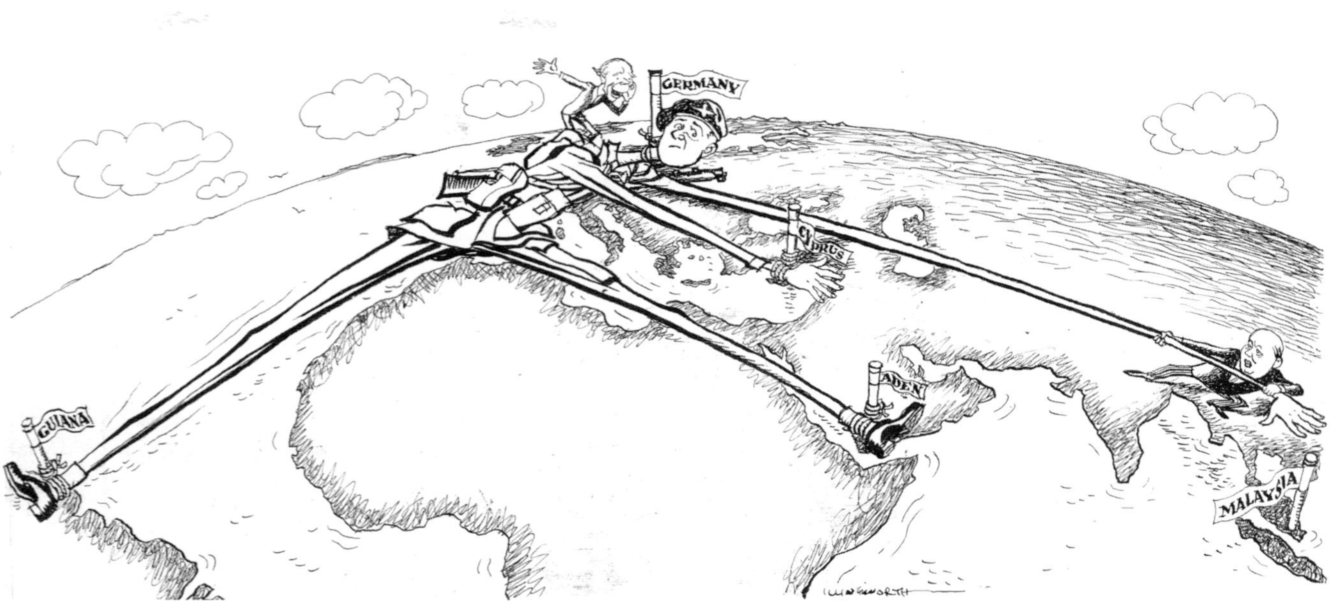

"CAREFUL! DON'T BREAK HIM."

'What shall we discuss first – Cyprus, Indonesia or the Beatles?'

above

6 January 1964

Defence Minister Peter Thornycroft stated that Britain would honour her commitments to Malaysia with enough British troops to meet any possible aggression from Indonesia. Despite the decline of the British Empire, the Army, stretched to its limits, was still deployed around the world, fighting colonial wars in Aden, Cyprus, Guiana and Malaya. The British Army also had a large deployment of troops remaining in West Germany to face the threat of a Soviet invasion.

10 February 1964

On 12 February, Prime Minister Douglas-Home visited President Johnson at the White House where they had a slight fall out over the mundane issue of the sale of British buses to Cuba. On 7 February, the Beatles had arrived at New York's newly renamed John F Kennedy Airport and were greeted by a crowd of 3,000 fans. On 9 February, they made their first live American television appearance on *The Ed Sullivan Show*. Approximately 74 million viewers, about half of the American population, watched the group perform on the show.

22 April 1964
Both the United States and the Soviets proposed cuts in the production of nuclear weapons. The most visible achievements on arms control by the superpowers were the conclusion of the Outer Space Treaty (1967) and the Nuclear Non-Proliferation Treaty (1968).

Slow Strip

27 May 1964
On 13 March 1946, David Low had created the TUC Carthorse to symbolise the trade unions. This representation is still popular today with British cartoonists.

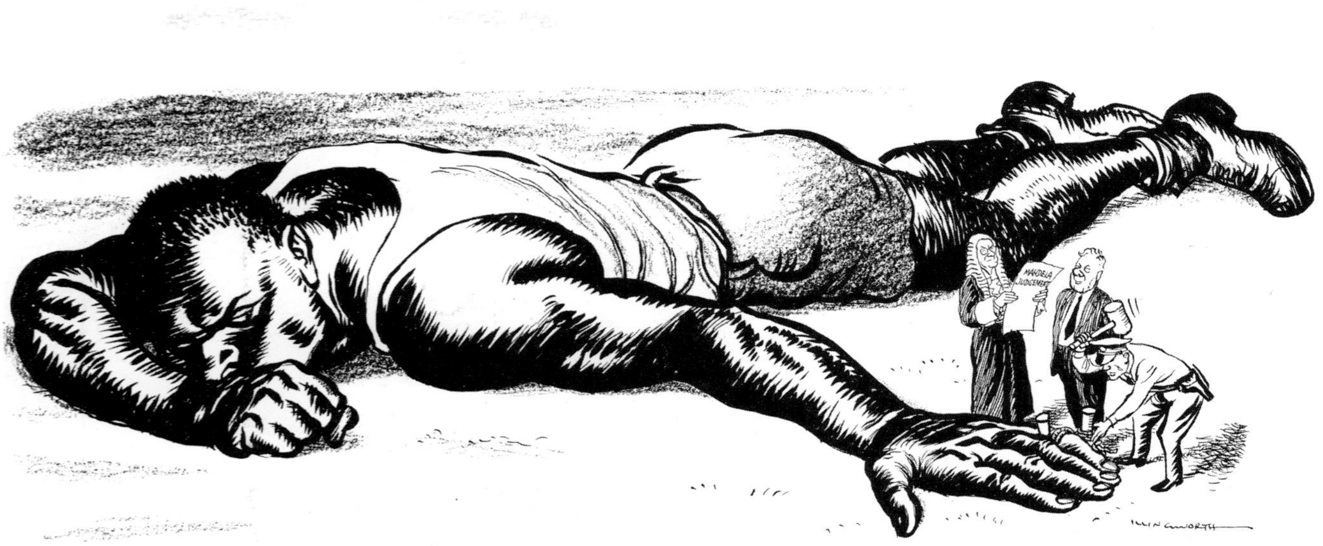

"There, I think that'll hold him"

The Warhead...

above
15 June 1964
On 12 June the leader of the anti-apartheid struggle in South Africa, Nelson Mandela, was jailed for life for sabotage. He told the court: "I do not deny that I planned sabotage. I did not plan it in a spirit of recklessness nor because I have any love of violence. I planned it as a result of a calm and sober assessment of the political situation that had arisen after many years of tyranny, exploitation and oppression of my people by the whites."

17 July 1964
During the 1964 Presidential elections President Johnson succeeded in painting his opponent, Republican Senator Barry Goldwater of Arizona, as a right-winger who might plunge the United States into nuclear warfare with the Soviet Union. In his most famous verbal gaffe, Goldwater once joked that the US military should "lob one (a nuclear bomb) into the men's room of the Kremlin".

24 July 1964
In the lead up to the 1964 General Election, Labour under Harold Wilson was initially ahead in the opinion polls, but started to slip as Douglas Home's Conservatives fought back, helped by Chancellor of the Exchequer Reginald Maudling's 'run for growth' pre-election budget. With the two main parties running neck and neck as polling day approached, the result rested on a knife edge.

HAROLD, LOOK!

2 November 1964
Despite polls predicting that President Johnson would win a landslide victory in the following week's American election, he barnstormed across the United States with the 'frantic determination of an underdog who fights to the bitter end'. According to the *Daily Mail*, Johnson had in only 11 months in the White House established himself as a President of real stature. 'He understands how to appeal to Labour with social welfare measures and to big business with economy cuts in Government spending. The paper also described him as one of the most formidable campaigners of all time.

LBJ shakes them all… and not just the hands but Americans too

23 March 1965
26 American bombers struck a North Vietnamese army camp with white phosphorous bombs. The camp which housed more than a battalion of Vietcong troops was reported to have become an inferno. It was the first bombing raid directed against troops and was the first time that the United States Air Force had used white phosphorus, which burns immediately on contact with air. In London, Canon Collins of St Paul's Cathedral, denounced American action in Vietnam and called on the British Government to oppose it.

'WE HAVE GOT A PERFECT COUNTRY HERE TODAY' – Mr Ian Smith, Prime Minister of Rhodesia

top
8 June 1965
320 luggage porters at Heathrow went on strike during the Whitsun bank holiday. Among the passengers stranded at the airport was Minister of Labour, Ray Gunter, sitting bottom left in the cartoon itself, who was due to address a Co-operative conference in Edinburgh. Gunter called the strike "a disgrace".

bottom
28 June 1965
White voters had overwhelmingly backed Prime Minister Ian Smith's Rhodesian Front in the May election. Smith had persuaded white Rhodesians that they could continue to defy world opinion indefinitely.
"I don't believe in black majority rule over Rhodesia," he proclaimed, "not in 1,000 years." Over 1,000 political detainees, the vast majority being ANC members, had been arrested and were being held without charge in detention camps.

LORD, FORGIVE THEM...

above

11 August 1965

The Federation of Malaysia was the name given to the 1963 political union of several British colonies on the Malay Peninsula, as well as Singapore and the island of Borneo. On 9 August, Singapore was expelled from the Malaysian Federation after declaring independence from Britain. The Malaysia Federation had been receiving military aid from Britain in its battle with Indonesia over the future of the island of Borneo.

16 August 1965

On 11 August, rioting broke out in Watts, an African American suburb of Los Angeles. The success of non-violent protests seemed irrelevant to many African Americans segregated and mired in poverty and despair in urban ghettoes. Fires raged for four days. Signs reading "Negro Owned" or "Owned by a Brother" protected some black businesses. Looting, violence and bloodshed intensified as rioters attacked whites, fought police, and shot at firefighters. Only after the National Guard sent soldiers to assist the police did peace return to Watts. The official death toll reached 34. News of Watts unleashed a series of riots and racial disturbances in other American cities.

top
27 August 1965
Illingworth always depicted the TUC General Secretary, George Woodcock, unflatteringly as a dinosaur. Unlike David Low's cart horse that sympathetically portrayed the TUC as being 'honest but simple-minded', Illingworth's visual metaphor simply implied that the trade unions were an outdated monster.

bottom
6 October 1965
On 27 July, Edward Heath beat off the favourite, Reginald Maudling, to win the Conservative leadership contest after Sir Alec Douglas-Home's resignation. The Labour Government's economic policy appeared indistinguishable from that of the previous Tory one. Malcolm Caldwell, a dedicated Labour campaigner, voiced the most extreme disillusionment in a letter to *Tribune*:

> Socialist principles have been tossed aside with almost indecent cynicism and casualness... Social welfare and economic development in Britain have been sacrificed to carry out a reactionary economic programme at the behest of international finance capital.

AND A HAPPIER NEW YEAR FOR ALL OF US

"Good to see old traditions kept up."

top
31 December 1965
President Johnson halted the bombing of North Vietnam in an attempt to pressure Ho Chi-Minh into a negotiated peace. The North Vietnamese denounced the bombing halt as a 'trick' and continued Viet Cong terrorist activities in the South.

bottom
17 January 1966
Tory Front Bench spokesman, Angus Maude, wrote in the *Spectator* that the Tory Party had "completely lost effective political leadership". This was backed up by former Tory MP Paul Williams, who stated that instead of being in a position to attack the Government, the Conservative Party had been "consumed with a host of committees studying largely irrelevant details of policy". Heath dismissed his critics by saying that "The Tory Party, must always remember, and as I am its leader I am determined it will remember, that it can never serve the nation by pandering to sectional interests."

2 March 1966
On 28 February, after returning from a trip to the Soviet Union, Wilson called a general election for 31 March. The *Pinky and Perky* show was, at the time, one of the most popular children's programmes on television. However, the pigs weren't just for kids as they often revealed a sharp eye for satire and ridicule. Indeed, BBC controllers attempted to withdraw an episode dealing with a mock election, fearing it might cause offence so near to the general election. But the viewing public quickly demanded its immediate reinstatement.

RETURN OF THE SCREW

ADVANTAGE BALL BOYS!

top
25 April 1966
On 31 March, Labour won the general election with the second largest majority in its history. Illingworth gives a negative spin to Chancellor of the Exchequer James Callaghan's preparations for his Budget on 3 May.

bottom
27 June 1966
Numerous left-wingers, led by Michael Foot, made demands in the House of Commons for assurances that British arms sold to the United States would not be used in Vietnam.

1 August 1966
The press had had a field day in 1964 when the then Prime Minister, Alec Douglas Home, had remarked casually that he used matchsticks to help him understand economic problems: "When I have to read economic documents I have to have a box of matches and start moving them into position to simplify and illustrate the points to myself." Now the tables appeared to have been turned as Wilson struggled to deal with the serious economic difficulties facing his government.

NEED A LIGHT?

22 August 1966
According to the *Daily Mail*, Verwoerd had effectively stamped out all forms of liberal expression in apartheid South Africa despite the booming economy. When South Africa left the Commonwealth in 1961, most South African exports had fallen to £400 million a year. In 1965 they had gone well over £500 million and were rising fast. On 6 September, Two weeks after this cartoon was published, Verwoerd was assassinated.

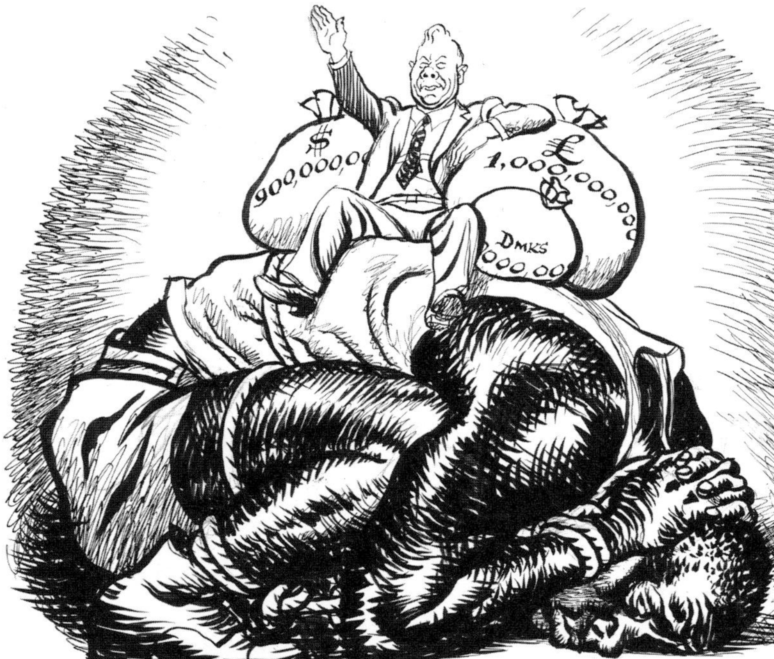

FULL BELLY, EMPTY HEART AND CONSCIENCE IN THE DEEP FREEZE

NOT IN FRONT OF THE CHILDREN

top
31 October 1966
At 9:15am on 21 October, 144 people, 116 of them children, were killed when a tip of coal waste slid onto the village of Aberfan in south Wales. On 26 October, a Tribunal was set up to inquire into the causes of the Aberfan disaster. There was controversy before the Tribunal had even begun. when the Attorney General warned about, and then imposed restrictions on, speculation in the press about the causes of the disaster. This, together with the accusations that earlier public enquiries into pit disasters were often whitewashes, exacerbated the already tense and difficult circumstances of the Tribunal.

bottom
25 Nov 1966
A new televised version of *Alice in Wonderland*, directed by Jonathan Miller, was shown at 9.05pm because Huw Weldon, Head of TV programmes felt it was, "unsuitable for children". Miller's fellow cast members of *Beyond the Fringe*, Peter Cook and Alan Bennett, played the Mad Hatter and the Mouse, respectively. The title role was played by Anne-Marie Mallik, the 13-year-old daughter of a Surrey barrister, this being her only known acting performance. The original of this cartoon was given to Huw Weldon

4 January 1967
Chairman Mao began the 'Down to the Countryside Movement'. Young intellectuals living in cities were ordered to go to the countryside. The term 'intellectuals' was actually used in the broadest sense to refer to recently graduated middle school students. This movement was in part a means of moving Red Guards from the cities to the countryside, where they would cause less social disruption. The Cultural Revolution in China was a period of widespread social and political upheaval that led to nationwide chaos and economic disarray, which engulfed much of Chinese society between 1966 and 1976.

MAO TSE ALADDIN

14 April 1967
Franco tried to put pressure on the British over returning Gibraltar to Spain by banning airspace to British aircraft over the Island. In retaliation, the British Government called off talks that were going to be held with the Spanish about Gibraltar.

"If you know of a better 'ole got to it"

top
21 April 1967
An American spacecraft equipped with a tiny shovel for testing the lunar surface made a successful landing on the moon. Surveyor Three's miniature shovel was designed to scrape 18 inches into the Moon surface and relay pictures back to earth. It could also crush pieces of the moon and test the texture to see if it could support a full-size spacecraft. The spot where it landed was considered as a possible landing sight for American astronauts in 1969 or 1970. The cartoon is a pastiche of Bruce Bairnsfather's famous First World War cartoon which carried the same caption.

bottom
10 May 1967
A London art gallery had offered 500 guineas for a painting by five-year-old Lewis Lyons which was being exhibited at the Royal Academy's Summer Exhibition. Lewis had painted a watercolour called *Trees and Monkeys*, when he was three after a day at the Zoo. In the House of Commons, the Labour Government pledged that Commonwealth interests would be safeguarded if Britain joined the Common Market. However a large contingent of backbenches on both sides of the House, such as pictured here (*left to right*) Michael Foot, Robin Turton, Douglas Jay and Emmanuel Shinwell, were dead against joining the Common Market. Tory MP Robin Turton said in the debate that the Government's plans were "a betrayal of the principles of the Queen of Parliaments" whilst Michael Foot declared that "we must not be whipped into the Common Market – and I certainly do not propose to be."

29 May 1967
On 16 May, Nasser requested the withdrawal of the UN Emergency Force stationed in the Sinai. This was a direct violation of the conditions under which Israel had returned control of the Sinai to Egypt after the Suez Campaign. The UN Force was supposed to safeguard Israel from Egypt, which also illegally closed the Straits of Tiran. The government of Israel approached the Great Powers who had guaranteed the freedom of Israeli navigation. Britain and France reneged on their commitment. President Johnson attempted a diplomatic resolution but gained little support in the international community for his idea of a maritime force that would compel Egypt to open the waterway. The Six Day War broke out on 5 June.

" How distressing ; she used to be a friend of ours once, didn't she . . .? "

12 June 1967
At the end of the Six Day War, Israeli troops had taken territory from surrounding Arab states many times larger than Israel itself whilst uniting the holy city of Jerusalem for the first time since 1948. On 12 June the ceasefire line was set by UN observers along these milestones. Meanwhile, Radio Cairo had been reporting that American and British troops had been fighting on Israel's side. The Egyptian newspaper *Al-Ahram* made a number of claims, among them that US and British carrier-based aircraft flew sorties against the Egyptians; that US aircraft based in Libya attacked Egypt; and that American spy satellites provided imagery to Israel. Many Arabs, who refused to accept that their armies were outclassed by the far superior Israeli military, were willing to believe in such tales.

FULL CIRCLE
Glassboro 1967, with apologies to Gillray, 1805

25 YEARS AFTER...

top
26 June 1967
President Johnson and the Soviet Union Foreign Minister Aleksei Kosygin met at Glassboro State College in Glassboro, New Jersey. The generally amicable atmosphere of the summit was referred to as the 'Spirit of Glassboro', although the leaders failed to reach agreement on limiting anti-ballistic missile systems. President Johnson stated that the talks had "made the world a little less dangerous". "Meetings like these," said the President, "don't of themselves make peace in the world. But it does help a lot to sit down and look a man in the eye and try to reason with him and particularly if he is trying to reason with you."

bottom
12 January 1968
It had been announced that the British Government intended to withdraw British forces from Singapore. In February 1942 Japanese troops had used bicycles to speed their advance on Singapore.

6 September 1967
The British public and the trade unions were taken aback by an increase in the cost of electricity.

Anybody seen my economic policy?
The electricity board seem to have pulled the plug out

PEACE OVERTURE

2 February 1968
President Johnson had been seeking ways to 'de-escalate' the conflict in Vietnam. At the end of January, however, the Viet Cong launched the Tet offensive, the largest military operation yet conducted by either side up to that point in the war. Eighty thousand Vietcong troops attacked more than 100 towns and cities, including the capital. The initial Vietcong attacks stunned allied forces and took them by surprise, but most were quickly contained and beaten back, inflicting massive casualties on the communists. Although the offensive was a military disaster for Vietcong forces, it had a profound effect on the American Administration and shocked the American public, which had been led to believe by its political and military leaders that the communists were, due to previous defeats, incapable of launching such a massive effort.

25 March 1968
Robert Kennedy, among others, had announced his intention to stand in the 1968 Presidential election by mid-March, and it was assumed that Johnson would also run – having won a landslide victory in 1964. In Illingworth's cartoon, he is seen lining up alongside Kennedy, with Nixon getting to run for the Republicans on the right of the drawing. However, on 31 March, LBJ announced that he would not be running.

'Don't look now, I think we're being followed.'

above
18 July 1968
In January, Alexander Dubcek had replaced Antonin Novotny as First Secretary of the Czechoslovak Communist Party and had initiated a programme of wide-ranging democratic reforms. These became known as the 'Prague Spring', and inevitably elicited opposition from the Soviet Union and other satellite states in Eastern Europe. In July, Warsaw Pact forces began a series of manoeuvres in Czechoslovakia, followed the next month by a full scale invasion that led to the removal of Dubcek and the end of the Czech revolution.

24 April 1968
On 20 April, Enoch Powell made his notorious speech in Birmingham, in which he predicted dire consequences as the result of immigration: "As I look ahead, I am filled with foreboding; like the Roman, I seem to see 'the River Tiber foaming with much blood'." The speech led to his sacking from the shadow cabinet, ending his hopes of a post in a future Conservative Government. However, thousands of workers staged strikes and marches in support of his views and he was inundated with letters from well wishers.

31 May 1968
With 8 million workers on strike, and riots in all the major French cities after three weeks of disruption, De Gaulle made a televised address on 24 May in which he demanded that the French people back his programme of reform or accept his resignation. But in the wake of this, the protests got worse, with more than 400 demonstrations in all parts of the country. On 29 May, De Gaulle left Paris (some said fled), but returned on 30 May to announce a general election, after which the protests started to peter out. (see Franklin cartoon on page 24 on De Gaulle's threat to resign)

Resign? Moi?

23 September 1968
In the hope of finding favour with the section of the Conservative Party that sympathised with Enoch Powell's views on immigration, Heath stated that a future Conservative Government would severely curtail the number of immigrants entering Britain.

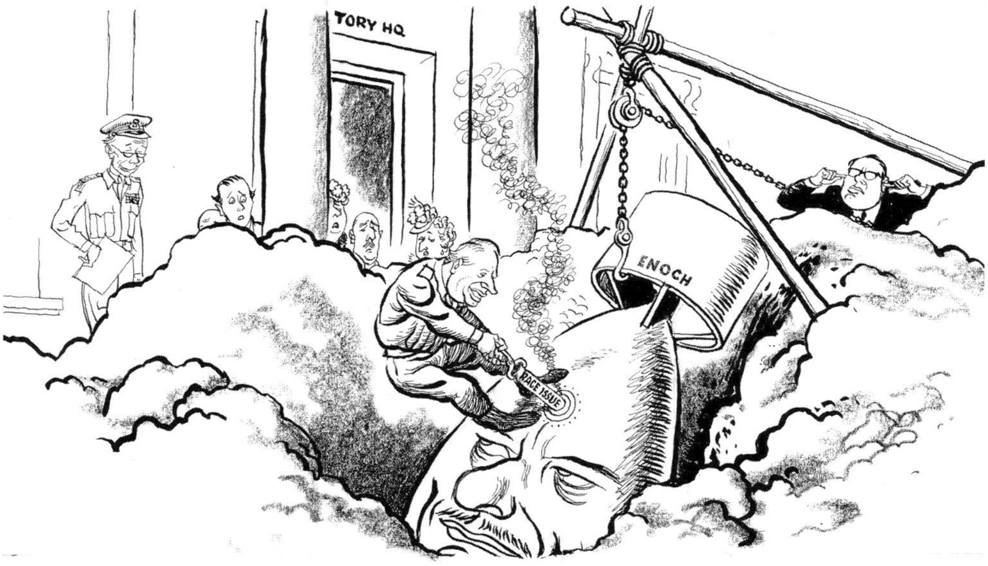

DE-FUSED?

28 October 1968
On 27 October, approximately 25,000 people took part in an anti-Vietnam War protest march in London organised by the Vietnam Solidarity Campaign. Trouble flared in Grosvenor Square, when an estimated 6,000 marchers led by the Maoist Britain-Vietnam Solidarity Front, broke away from the main march, and confronted 1,000 policemen outside the United States Embassy. The protesters charged at the police wall but failed to break through. After three hours of stalemate they all dispersed.

The change of wind

13 January 1969
On the day this cartoon was published, Asian traders were told to quit the Western Province of Zambia. After political independence, many African states began an anti-Asian trend that led to the expulsion of tens of thousands of Asians. In Kenya, Malawi and Tanzania, to avoid economic disruptions, Asians were forced out gradually. In Uganda, however, they were expelled more quickly and dramatically. When Idi Amin took over Uganda in 1971, he simply ordered all Asians out of the country, forcing 80,000 of them to leave without their assets. In 1968 there were 345,000 Asians residents in Kenya, Tanzania, Zambia, Malawi, and Uganda. By 1984, their numbers had fallen to about 85,000.

WALSALL CONCERTO

27 January 1969
The previous year, Enoch Powell had made his 'rivers of blood' speech, warning that uncontrolled immigration would change Britain irrevocably. Heath had sacked Powell from his post as Shadow Defence Secretary, telling him that the speech was "racialist in tone and liable to exacerbate racial tensions". However, on 25 January, Heath joined Powell on the platform, giving a speech to a Conservative rally in Walsall on immigration, which according to Harold Wilson's diaries, "...in all but his choice of words recalling the thoughts of Enoch Powell".

17 February 1969
In January a Czech student, Jan Palach, had burned himself to death in protest at the Soviet invasion of Czechoslovakia the previous year. Walter Ulbricht, the East German leader had just returned to Berlin from meetings with Soviet Premier Brezhnev, with instructions not to allow dissent to spread into East Germany.

14 April 1969
Secretary of State for Employment Barbara Castle tried to introduce a programme of industrial relations reform limiting the power of the trade unions. The controversial white paper, 'In Place of Strife' faced stiff opposition from the Trades Union Congress and some key cabinet ministers, such as James Callaghan, and the proposals were shelved. This episode proved politically damaging for Wilson, whose approval ratings fell to 26%; the lowest for any Prime Minister since polling began. In hindsight, many have argued that the failure of the unions to adopt the proposals of 'In Place of Strife', led to the far more drastic curbs on trade union power under Margaret Thatcher in the 1980s. Opposition leader Edward Heath bought his first yacht *Morning Cloud* in 1969 and won the Sydney to Hobart boat race that year.

PUTTING THE OTHER BOOT IN

7 July 1969
To Illingworth, it seemed that too many people were only too willing to overlook military dictatorship, violence and corruption in Black Africa while condemning Rhodesian society which, whatever its shortcomings, offered relative security for its citizens. For example, on 30 June, the Nigerian Government banned all Red Cross aid to Biafra during the civil war which led to more than 1 million people either dying in battle or from starvation. On 5 July, Tom Mboya, President Jomo Kenyatta's Minister for Economic Planning, was assassinated. Although a suspect was arrested, tried and subsequently hanged, there were claims at the time that Kenyatta was behind the assassination.

25 August 1969
The 'Troubles' in Northern Ireland had begun the previous year with rioting continuing throughout 1969. During this time, Catholics had complained about the violent methods used by the Royal Ulster Constabulary, and in particular an auxiliary force known as the 'B' Specials. Home Secretary Jim Callaghan launched an inquiry into the riots, which led to the abolition of the 'B' specials. In August, in response to the rapidly deteriorating public order situation, the Army was called in to aid the civil power. On 22 August, Callaghan visited Ulster.

FORWARD THE 'C' SPECIALS

29 September 1969
Labour's 1969 Conference in Blackpool was less stormy than earlier ones, partly because of improved economic performance, but also because a General Election was expected shortly. After devaluation in November 1967, austerity measures successfully restored the balance of payments to a £40 million surplus. Illingworth's use of the Doodlebug carrying Wilson was a good visual metaphor, because just before the 1970 General Election the balance of payments turned into a small deficit. This was announced just before polling and is often cited as one of the reasons for Labour's defeat.

LOOK, NO HANDS!

1 December 1969
The My Lai Massacre was the mass murder of hundreds of unarmed villagers in South Vietnam, most of them women and children, by American soldiers on 16 March 1968. Some of the victims were sexually abused, beaten, tortured or maimed, and some of the bodies were found mutilated. The US military codeword for the My Lai hamlet was Pinkville. The incident prompted widespread outrage around the world. The massacre also reduced support at home in the United States for the Vietnam War. In November 1969, General William Peers was appointed to conduct a thorough investigation into the My Lai incident and its subsequent cover-up. Of the 26 US soldiers initially charged with criminal offences for their actions at My Lai, only one was convicted.

Other books published by The Political Cartoon Society

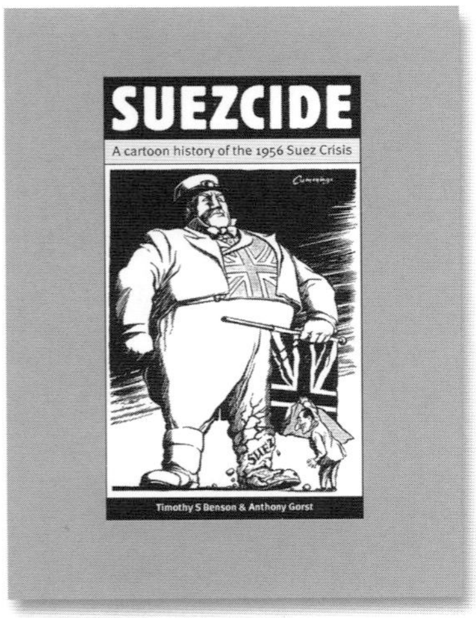

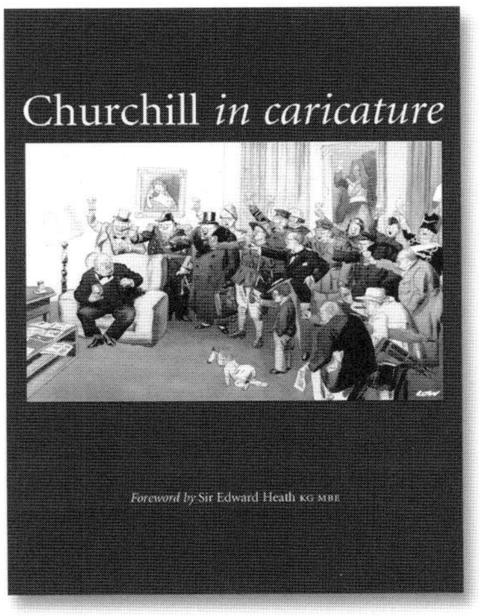

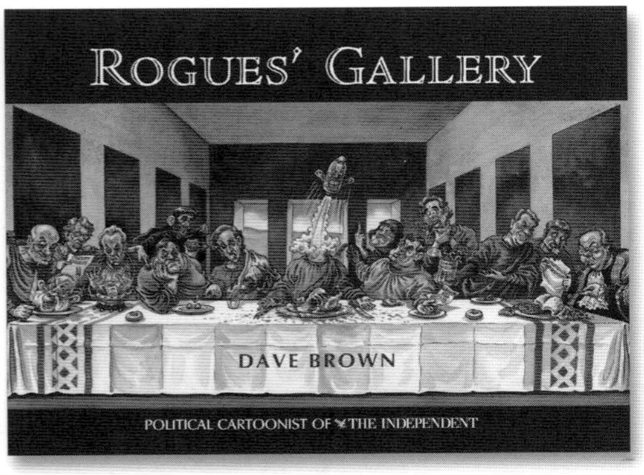

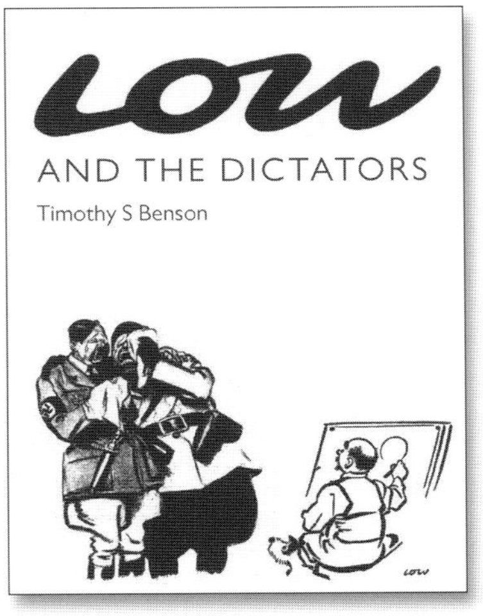

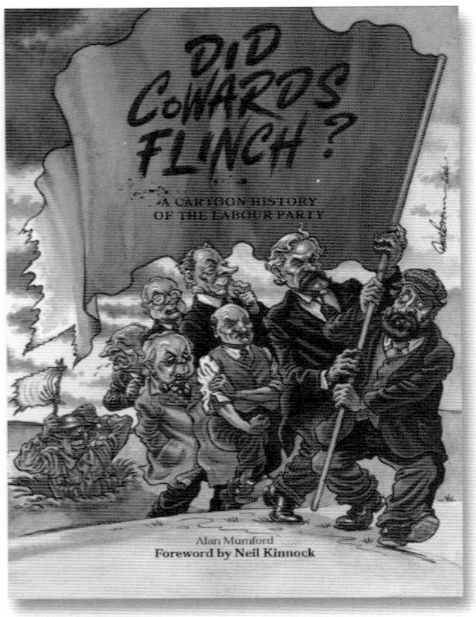

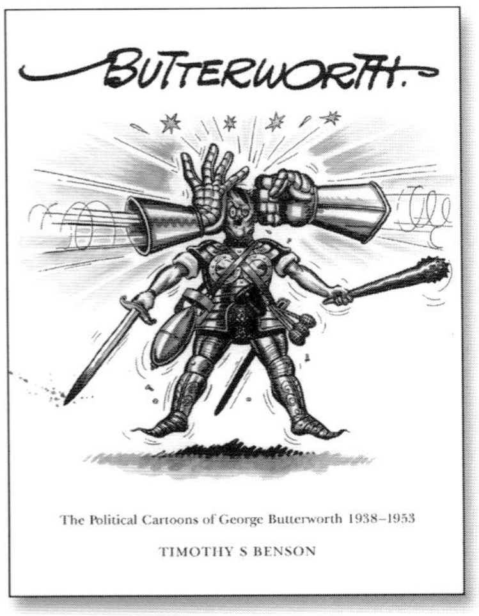

32 Store Street, London WC1E 7BS, 020 7580 1114
www.politicalcartoon.co.uk